Men Are from Earth, Women Are from Earth

DEVELOPMENTS IN CLINICAL PSYCHIATRY

A Series of Books Edited By
Anthony L. LaBruzza, M.D.

The books in this series address various facets of the role of psychiatry in the modern world.

Using DSM-IV: *A Clinician's Guide to Psychiatric Diagnosis*
Anthony L. LaBruzza and José M. Méndez-Villarrubia

Filicide: *The Murder, Humiliation, Mutilation, Denigration, and Abandonment of Children by Parents*
Arnaldo Rascovsky

Return from Madness: *Psychotherapy with People Taking the New Antipsychotic Medications and Emerging from Severe, Lifelong, and Disabling Schizophrenia*
Kathleen Degen and Ellen Nasper

The Chambers of Memory: *PTSD in the Life Stories of U. S. Vietnam Veterans*
H. William Chalsma

Winning Cooperation from Your Child! *A Comprehensive Method to Stop Defiant and Aggressive Behavior in Children*
Kenneth Wenning

Brainstorms: *Understanding and Treating the Emotional Storms of Attention Deficit Hyperactivity Disorder from Childhood through Adulthood*
H. Joseph Horacek

Twisted: *Inside the Mind of a Drug Addict*
Carl Adam Richmond

The Essential Internet:
A Guide for Psychotherapists and Other Mental Health Professionals
Anthony L. LaBruzza

Building a Neuropsychology Practice:
A Guide to Respecialization
Marvin H. Podd and Donald P. Seelig

Men Are from Earth, Women Are from Earth:
A Guide to Winning Cooperation from Your Spouse
Kenneth Wenning

Men Are from Earth, Women Are from Earth

A GUIDE TO WINNING COOPERATION FROM YOUR SPOUSE

Kenneth Wenning, Ph.D.

JASON ARONSON INC.
Northvale, New Jersey
London

Production Editor: Elaine Lindenblatt

This book was set in 12 pt. Fairfield Light by Alpha Graphics of Pittsfield, NH, and printed and bound by Book-mart Press, Inc. of North Bergen, NJ.

Library of Congress Cataloging-in-Publication Data

Wenning, Kenneth,
    Men are from Earth, women are from Earth : a guide to winning
cooperation from your spouse / Kenneth Wenning.
        p.   cm.
    Includes bibliographical references and index.
    ISBN 0-7657-0102-2 (alk. paper)
    1. Communication in marriage.   2. Interpersonal communication.
3. Man-woman relationships.   I. Title.
HQ734.W4856   1998
646.7'8—dc21   97-18707

Printed in the United States of America on acid-free paper. For information and catalog write to Jason Aronson Inc., 230 Livingston Street, Northvale, NJ 07647-1726. Or visit our website: http://www.aronson.com

To my wife
Leslie

℘ Contents ℘

✤ Preface ✤

The screaming matches that many men and women experience are often wrongly described as the "battle between the sexes," as if there were something inherently adversarial, explosive, or unstable in male–female relationships. Nothing could be further from the truth, as evidenced by the fact that many male and female humans live together happily and cooperatively, and many gay individuals have great difficulty getting along with their same-sex partners. Since gender differences do not cause male–female fighting, how then do we explain this so-called battle between the sexes? The answer lies in something that is inherently human, not inherently male or female. In my view the primary cause of relational disturbance among all humans is our self-defeating tendency to cling tenaciously to irrational beliefs about love partners and our extraordinary talent for engaging in unattractive relationship-damaging behaviors and attitudes when frustrated by our mates.

Men Are from Earth, Women Are from Earth is a self-help book for couples in conflict. Its primary goal is to help couples stop fighting and start living together cooperatively—like true partners in life. Toward this end the following chapters show married individuals how to overcome their self-defeating relationship-damaging attitudes and behaviors, identify and prevent the main cause of emotional disturbance in marriage, and win greater cooperation from their mates. This book also teaches couples effective communication and problem-solving skills for the peaceful resolution of disputes and conflicts. In a nutshell, the problem-solving methods described in this book constitute a prescription that women and men can use to end, once and for all, their marital battles and find greater pleasure in married life.

In writing this book I was influenced by the work of a number of skilled psychotherapists. Most notably I am indebted to Albert Ellis, Ph.D., whose work has significantly improved my effectiveness as a therapist. I also thank Raymond DiGiuseppe, Ph.D., Joyce Sichel, Ph.D., Raymond Yeager, Ph.D., Dominic DiMattia, Ed.D., Matthew McKay, Ph.D., Patrick Fanning, Kim Paleg, Ph.D., Windy Dryden, Ph.D., Michael Bloomquist, Ph.D., and Paul Hauck, Ph.D. Their contributions to the literature on relational disorders have greatly increased my ability to understa d and help troubled couples.

For their help in the production of this book, I want to thank several members of the team at Jason Aronson Inc. Specifically, many thanks go to Michael Moskowitz, Ph.D., Norma Pomerantz, Elaine Lindenblatt, Judith Tulli, and

Rosanna Mazzei. It has been a pleasure working with them on this project. I also thank Patricia Nann for her skill in preparing the original manuscript and my wife Leslie, not only for her love and support but also for her helpful feedback on some of the ideas expressed in the following pages.

CHAPTER

1

☙

*Getting Ready
for Change*

*A*ny marriage can work as long as both individuals are willing to do what it takes to make it work. The goal of this chapter is to help you prepare for the changes you will need to make to increase your chances of improving or saving your marriage. To prepare for change, you need to learn six facts about men, women, and marriage, know the difference between marital disturbance and marital dissatisfaction, learn the four common behaviors that destroy marriage, and practice several preliminary techniques to start improving your marriage today.

SIX FACTS ABOUT MEN, WOMEN, AND MARRIAGE

Fact #1: Men Are from Earth! Women Are from Earth!

Surprised? I know this concept stands in contrast to a current popular view of males and females as beings so entirely different that they are thought to have come from separate planets. Contrary to that point of view, this book rests on the assumption that, as Earthlings, men and women are more alike than different. Although it is important to understand the disparities between women and men, the key to a healthier and more mutually satisfying marital relationship lies in your ability to see beyond superficial gender distinctions and to concentrate on the numerous ways in which you and your partner are similar to each other. By focusing on similarities rather than differences, you and your spouse will move toward the common ground upon which a strong marriage can be developed and maintained.

How are men and women alike? As Earthlings, most average men and women want: cooperation, love, support, fair and considerate treatment, and companionship and loyalty from a husband or wife; children to love, protect, and nurture; a steady and secure source of income; reasonably nice living space; good food; time to pursue activities for personal development or recreation; time to play together; a satisfying love/sex relationship; maximal pleasure from life and minimal frustration and pain; a nice group of friends with whom to interact; and a satisfying work environment. Men and women also generally do not want to get sick or die, experience physical pain, lose a loved one, feel alone in life, live without love and sex, receive disapproval or inconsiderate treatment from others, do boring work, pay high taxes, or pay expensive psychotherapy bills. As you can see, in all of these areas and many others, men and women share many common hopes, desires, and fears. Much common ground indeed!

Men and women also show a similar ability to engage in self-defeating behaviors and/or to cling devoutly to irrational (unhelpful) beliefs about themselves, others, and the world. Both sexes are equally capable of displaying dysfunctional behaviors such as yelling, pouting, whining, or blaming and thinking irrational thoughts such as "My husband absolutely *must* do what I say," or "I *need* love and approval from my wife," or "I *can't stand* that husband of mine." Males and females are also equally capable of continuing to use self-sabotaging behavior and thinking even when it is clear that such behavior and thinking become a major turnoff to others, especially the spouse. As humans, however, men and women also have an equally well-developed ability to think about their thinking and behavior and to change *both* if they *choose* to.

Despite these areas of similarity, there are undeniable differences between men and women. Male and female bodies are obviously anatomically different in some respects, although even anatomically men and women are more alike than different. Religious, cultural, familial, and parental influences on young males and females also often lead to gender-specific differences in worldview, values, priorities, attitudes, and behaviors that require mutual respect, understanding, and tolerance. In my view, however, all the differences between men and women—indeed among all the world's people—represent beautiful but largely superficial variations of the basic human being. Men and women who become overly focused on male/female differences prevent themselves from sharing, connecting, and relating at our core human level. Only secondarily is your partner male, female, black, white, Asian, Hindu, Jewish, Christian, and so forth. Your spouse is first and foremost a human being!

Fact #2: The Ideal or Perfect Marriage Does Not Exist

To give your marriage the best chance of working and to increase the chances that you will be able to encourage greater cooperation from your spouse, you need to give up idealized notions that good marriages are constantly filled with love, romance, cooperation, intensity, and excitement. Why? Because no one, including your spouse, will ever be able to live up to perfectionistic ideas about marriage. Faced with demands for a perfect relationship your spouse will begin to resent you and believe that no matter what he or she does it will never be good enough for you. Your partner may then begin to think, "I can never please that husband/wife of mine, so why should I bother to do anything. To hell with it. I'll just do what I want to make myself feel better." Paradoxically, by being more tolerant of your partner's fallibility, you will probably get more—though not all—of what you want out of your marriage. But it will take hard work on your part, which includes maintaining a realistic, nonutopian view of marriage. All marriages have ups and downs.

Fact #3: Good Intentions Alone Will Not Fix Your Marriage or Help You Win Cooperation from Your Spouse

Your good intentions and hopes for a better relationship with your husband or wife represent a good starting point on your journey toward a better marriage. But as you already know, the road to hell is paved with good intentions. Unless you're prepared to take those good intentions, hopes, and desires and convert them into an action plan, that is, to use those positive feelings to produce new *love behaviors* and attitudes toward your spouse, you will likely passively pine away while your marriage goes up in flames. As noted psychologist and marriage counselor Paul Hauck (1984) says, people really love what their spouses *do* for them in relation to their deepest desires and needs.

What are love behaviors? Love behaviors are concrete actions that *you* produce to reassure your partner of your love, loyalty, and support, and that lighten your husband's or wife's load in life. Love behaviors represent your love in *action!* To make your marriage work you need to be prepared to display *many* love behaviors toward your partner.

Fact #4: To Win Cooperation from Your Spouse, You First Need to Take Full Responsibility for Your Emotional and Behavioral Actions and Reactions

This is a critically important point. Mature, psychologically healthy individuals are generally able to understand that they are personally responsible for their emotional and behavioral responses toward other people or toward frustrating situations. Stated somewhat differently, your spouse does not cause you to become deeply depressed, panicked, or enraged. You enrage, depress, or panic yourself based on the way you think about or evaluate problems with your husband or wife. In Chapter 2 you will learn a great deal more about this key insight. For now just keep in mind the idea that you control your thoughts, your emotions, your words, the tone of your voice, and your body and its behaviors. When you yell, scream, nag, slam doors, throw things, pout, sulk, mope, or stomp out of the house, nobody but you creates these self-defeating reactions. If you do not accept responsibility for your emotional and behavioral actions and reactions, you will continue to insist that your spouse or others *cause* you to flare up in anger or act in immature ways. Thus, you will keep trying to control others or your spouse in order to control yourself. Trying to control others to control yourself is a strategy that will make your problems worse rather than better.

Fact #5: If You Can't Win Cooperation from Your Spouse, the Two of You Were Not Meant To Be Together

You did not get married to be alone, have no sex life, do all or most of the work around the house, raise the kids by yourself, or put up with abusive or irresponsible behavior by your husband or wife. Quite the opposite, in fact. You married to have a partner in life—a soul mate, lover, and best friend with whom you could share life's joys and sorrows. If you use all the techniques discussed in this book, and still get no cooperation from your partner, you have several options: (1) Encourage your partner to enter marital counseling with you. (2) If your partner refuses to join you in marital counseling and you still don't know what to do, you might seek individual therapy for yourself to figure out how best to deal with an unhappy marriage.

(3) Accept the fact that your spouse probably will never change, and try to live with it as best you can. (4) Accept that the two of you weren't meant for each other, and move on to a new and hopefully more satisfying relationship.

Fact #6: Real Love Delivers Attitudes of Support, Compassion, Loyalty, and Behaviors That Demonstrate Love

If you profess to love your spouse but largely do nothing to demonstrate or prove your love, you are *not* really in love. Again, people who are really in love demonstrate *love behavior* frequently toward the loved partner. Real love delivers kind and considerate behavior and attitudes of patience, understanding, and support toward your husband or wife. Real love helps you to help your husband or wife achieve his or her goals in life—*not yours!*

MARITAL DISSATISFACTION VS. MARITAL DISTURBANCE

Dr. Albert Ellis and Dr. Windy Dryden (1997), two internationally renowned psychologists who have shown thousands of people how to gain relief from emotional suffering, have noted that marital dissatisfaction occurs when husband and/or wife are not receiving enough of what they want from each other and from the marital relationship. Individuals can become dissatisfied over such things as insufficient affection, companionship, sex, or support from husband or wife, or over areas of disagreement such as how to budget money or where to go for vacation. Dissatisfaction can also develop in relation to irresponsible behavior on the part of one or both individuals such as not being able to hold a job, abusing drugs or alcohol, or staying out all night and not telling your partner where you are. Marital dissatisfactions lead naturally to appropriate feelings of concern, frustration, moderate anger, and/or disappointment, but not to dysfunctional emotions such as rage, deep depression, or severe anxiety.

Marital disturbance develops when husband or wife or both horrify, enrage, depress, panic, or shock themselves about one or several areas of dissatisfaction (Ellis and Dryden 1997). For example, a husband may depress himself over a wife's not spending as much time with him as he demands or a wife may enrage herself over an inconsiderate husband who repeatedly leaves dirty clothes on the floor. Individuals may also disturb themselves over more serious dissatisfactions such as extramarital affairs, substance abuse, points of disagreement, verbal abuse, or other forms of irresponsible behavior by the spouse. Though situations such as these are truly undesirable and frustrating, you do not have to become emotionally disturbed about them. (In Chapter 2 you will learn a great deal more about how to become a thoroughly undisturbable individual.) If you are in a state of marital disturbance, it means that you have become emotionally disturbed about your marital dissatisfactions and that you are taking your marital dissatisfactions, whatever they may be, too seriously. Marital disturbance is unhealthy and needs to be eliminated before you try to solve problems with your mate. Marital disturbance, that is, feeling and acting crazy over mild to severe dissatisfactions, also prevents you and your partner from making good judgments about whether your marriage is viable. Also, when you are feeling or acting crazy you are overwhelmed by self-defeating emotions such as rage, panic, shock, or deep depression and are therefore unable to think or act in self-helping ways or to come up with reasonable problem-solving methods.

When a couple comes to me with marital disturbance, I first help husband and wife stop disturbing themselves over their respective areas of dissatisfaction. Once the emotional and behavioral disturbance has been eliminated or significantly reduced, the couple can then sanely begin to examine and discuss areas of dissatisfaction with the goal of reducing or minimizing these areas of dissatisfaction and increasing areas of satisfaction within the marriage. If change does not occur and the dissatisfactions persist, one or both partners may then rationally decide to end the relationship and perhaps even part on reasonably friendly terms with only appropriate sadness and regret over a relationship that did not work out. Too bad. That's the way it sometimes goes.

BEHAVIORS AND ATTITUDES
THAT DESTROY MARRIAGE

This section covers four major "turnoff" behaviors and attitudes that are likely to repulse your mate and influence him or her to be even more uncooperative about solving problems and/or meeting your deepest desires and needs. As you review the following topics be totally honest with yourself.

Admitting that you engage in one or several of the following behaviors does not mean that you are a bad person or that your point of view about your marital problems is wrong. It simply means that you are a fallible human being who sometimes acts in self-defeating ways. It also means that you can then target and work to eliminate specific self-defeating behaviors and attitudes and by so doing increase your chances of solving problems with your partner.

Blaming and Insulting Your Spouse

Angrily blaming, attacking, and insulting your partner is a definite turnoff and, if you think about it, rarely solves your marital problems. For example, how many times have you yelled at or insulted your husband or wife and encountered the following reaction? "Gee honey, your accusations and insults really help me see how wrong I've been in so many ways. I'm so very sorry and promise to do things your way from now on." If your partner does react this way, he or she probably *is* from another planet. Most people when attacked or insulted react by saying something like, "Drop dead!"

If you have been blaming, insulting, and angrily criticizing your spouse, now is the time to admit that this approach has only made your marital relationship worse. If you need further proof, the next time you start to verbally attack your partner quickly run to the bathroom mirror and look at yourself. Do you think that red face, bulging eyes, loud voice, and self-righteous attitude make you attractive to your partner? Would you want to sit down and discuss a problem with someone who looks and sounds the way you do when you enrage yourself over some area of marital dissatisfaction?

If hopefully you have concluded that blaming and insulting your spouse is part of the problem, you will then have greater motivation to give this up and instead focus on non-inflammatory ways of communicating your concerns. By presenting your worries, fears, frustrations, and disappointments to your spouse in non-blaming, gentler ways, you stand a better chance of being heard, understood, and responded to. Remember, though, there are never any guarantees that you will absolutely get what you want from your husband or wife.

 The Silent Treatment

Many humans use this type of immature behavior to quietly torture a spouse in retaliation for being hurt, frustrated, or disappointed in some way and to manipulate him or her into begging for forgiveness. Although the silent treatment and/ or pouting may work once in a while, over time it may lead your partner to see you as an insecure, psychologically weak person who acts like a 3-year-old when something happens that you don't like. It is also likely that your spouse will start to resent the pleading-for-forgiveness ritual you demand before agreeing to end your silent pouting. In short, the pouting/silent treatment approach to problem solving is generally self-defeating, earns you a reputation of being a baby, and rarely solves your problem. Furthermore, at the time you are delivering the silent treatment to your spouse, you are probably suffering silently while you pretend that he or she does not exist.

The self-helping alternative to the pouting is to assertively (not aggressively) offer your spouse a clear, direct statement about the problem you would like to solve and how you feel about it not being solved (e.g., worried, frustrated, sad, annoyed). You can also ask when your spouse would be willing to meet with you to discuss the problem that you are concerned about. Your partner can then choose to respond in a mature and levelheaded manner or respond to your appropriate assertiveness with a display of immature, self-defeating, irresponsible behavior of his or her own. If your partner reacts in an infantile manner, at least it will be your partner acting that way—not you. In later chapters you will learn much more about how to cope with immature behavior by your spouse and how to influence him or her to grow up and cooperate. For now just work on displaying mature, honest, non-blaming, non-manipulative behaviors on your part. Regardless of whether the straightforward, honest, and mature approach helps your spouse to listen and cooperate, it will definitely make you attractive to many other people.

Getting Stoned, High, or Drunk to Cope with Frustration in Your Marriage

Turning to chemicals to numb the psychological pain of frustration, anger, disappointment, depression, or anxiety related to a marital problem is one of the most self-defeating behaviors you could possibly engage in. First, you will be starting down a slippery slope toward chemical addiction or abuse that will ruin your physical and mental health and leave your loved ones, especially your children, scared, embarrassed, and angry at your irresponsible behavior. Second, when stoned or drunk you are not able to think straight and in fact will often say and/or do things you will regret having done or said when you sober up. Third, your abuse of drugs or alcohol will give your spouse plenty of ammunition to use against you. Your spouse will accuse you of irresponsible behavior and of copping out by using drugs or alcohol. Finally, getting high as a coping strategy will stunt your psychological growth because the abuse of substances will prevent you from learning how to bear painful emotions like sadness, worry, anger, and frustration and how to utilize such feelings to seek creative solutions to your marital troubles.

If you have started down this road, stop right now before it's too late to stop on your own. If you have a drug and/or alcohol problem that is beyond your control, admit it and make appointments to see a physician for a medical evaluation and a licensed mental health professional for guidance on the proper treatment program for your substance abuse problem. Getting help now may prevent a great deal of misery and suffering later in your life and will increase your chances of improving your marriage and your relationship with your children.

Having an Extramarital Affair

Married individuals sometimes seek lovers as a way of coping with marital disturbance or dissatisfaction. Though it may seem exciting and wonderful at first, such behavior does nothing to enhance your marriage and in fact puts you at great risk of permanently damaging your relationship with your husband or wife when your affair is discovered.

In some cases the person having an affair knows that the marriage is shot, does not have the courage to tell the spouse that it's over, and consciously or unconsciously hopes the affair will be discovered so the spouse will make the decision to end the relationship. This is truly a cowardly way to end a marriage and will often greatly upset other family members and any children involved, as well as earn you a reputation as a bad person. If you truly believe there is no hope for your marriage, it is better to end it in a direct honest manner, try to part on friendly terms, and then move on to your next relationship. If, on the other hand, you still want your marriage to work out, stop the affair right now and work on fixing your marriage. If an affair has happened, it likely means that serious problems have developed between you and your mate, so consider the possibility of seeking individual therapy or joint therapy with a marriage counselor to help you solve your marital difficulties.

PRELIMINARY TIPS TO WIN COOPERATION FROM YOUR SPOUSE

To encourage your husband or wife to give you more of what you want, you need to make some changes first. Review the following five sections and *force* yourself to practice these behavioral tactics each day around your mate. By forcing some behavioral change in yourself, you will probably elicit a few positive responses from your spouse, and these new responses by him or her can lead you to have more positive thoughts and feelings about your partner. If initially you don't receive positive responses from your spouse, don't worry! It may take some time before you see any clear results. Again, by forcing yourself to display the following behaviors you will probably begin to think in new ways about your partner, because changes in your behavior can produce changes in your thinking and in your emotions. In Chapter 2 you will learn the reverse process—how to change your thinking in ways that will further support and strengthen positive self-helping behaviors and attitudes.

Before you begin to use the following techniques, it is critical that you promise yourself that you will work to transform yourself into the most attractive partner you can be, regardless of whether your spouse ever changes. By using attractive social skills, humor skills, communication, and problem-solving skills, you will become a more appealing person to your partner and to all who know you. If your partner does not respond to your self-improvement efforts, it will only be his or her loss.

1. *Give your husband or wife three compliments per day.* By paying attention to good behavior and thinking displayed by your spouse you may be able to encourage him or her to display better behaviors and attitudes more of the time. To be able to genuinely offer a few compliments to your mate, try to focus on the glass being half full, not half empty. I've counseled many married individuals who obsessively focused on what the spouse was doing wrong and seemed blind to what

the husband or wife was doing right. All human beings, even the most irresponsible and obnoxious ones, display some good behavior each day. If you search carefully, you will find positive behaviors and qualities in your mate. These might simply be things such as going to work each day, taking the trash out once a week, showing kindness to others, talking in a nice tone of voice, having a good idea about anything, wearing a nice outfit, or cooking a good meal. By focusing on your mate's positive behaviors and lightening up your attacks on his or her faults, you will almost certainly begin to capture your partner's attention, which is the first necessary step toward solving marital problems.

2. *Try to speak to your spouse with sincerity and kindness.* It has been said that "the great secret to success in life is sincerity—and if you can fake that, you've got it made!" It may not feel comfortable at first to act in a sincere manner, especially if there have been a lot of negative feelings building up toward your spouse. But by approaching your partner with sincerity as opposed to sarcasm or hostility, you will greatly improve your chances of being heard, understood, and hopefully responded to. Also keep in mind that changes in behavior can produce changes in thinking. You may find that if you practice sincerity routinely, it will start to become a real or genuine part of your personality. Any new behavior or attitude you try will feel awkward at first, but the more you practice new ways of relating to others, including your spouse, the easier and more natural it becomes. If by forcing yourself to act sincerely, you gradually become a more sincere person, you will definitely become more

attractive to many people, including your spouse. What have you got to lose?

Keep in mind that speaking kindly to your partner also helps to reduce anger and defensiveness and begins to create a calmer atmosphere within which problems can be discussed, examined, understood, and hopefully solved. Pick and choose your words carefully. Pretend you are an ambassador at an embassy in a foreign land and are charged with the responsibility of solving a delicate international problem. It is now imperative that you stay cool. Skilled diplomats always speak kindly and respectfully toward one another and never allow themselves to degenerate to the level of personal attacks on each other's character. To help you use kind words toward your spouse, tell yourself the following:

- My husband or wife is a fallible human being who does many things well but, like all humans, myself included, also makes many mistakes.
- My partner is always a worthwhile person though I may not like some of his or her irresponsible, obnoxious, or difficult behaviors and attitudes.
- I can talk to my spouse with kindness, respect, and sincerity about the behaviors and attitudes I don't like, while at the same time always supporting his or her worth as a person.

3.) *Be a good sport when your partner frustrates you.* Again at this stage you may need to push or force yourself to have what is known as high frustration tolerance (HFT)—that is, good-natured acceptance of frustrating situations. The advantage to you and to your marriage is that HFT prevents problems with your mate from escalating into major "blow-outs." For example, Jeff might discover that his car has almost no gas in it because his wife Maria was out running errands all day and forgot to fill the gas tank. He is frustrated and inconvenienced because he is running late for an evening meeting and now has to take the time to stop and get gas. In this example, Jeff could use HFT to accept (though not like) this frustrating situation, forgive his wife for being inconsiderate, and ask her to please remember to fill up the tank the next time she is out. On the other hand, he could give in to low frustration tolerance (LFT), tell himself that he *can't stand* this irresponsible behavior by his wife, start a fight with her over what an inconsiderate *jerk* she is, and in the process create increased tensions with, and elicit counterattacks from, Maria. Meanwhile, the car sits in the driveway with an empty gas tank. Ironically, Jeff is making himself even more late for his meeting because of the time he spends fighting with Maria, and he will likely arrive at his meeting in an agitated state. In Chapter 2 you will learn more about the irrational thoughts that create LFT and ways to develop and maintain a philosophy of HFT so that you never again have to become severely disturbed over anything. Again, as with sincerity, kindness, and respect, HFT will improve your image and attractiveness to others and hopefully to your spouse as well.

4. *Be playful and silly at times.* No one likes a grouch or a sourpuss—someone with no sense of humor. Grumpiness will likely do nothing but push your mate further away from

you. In other words, a chronic bad mood and lack of a sense of humor may bring your spouse down and motivate him or her to spend lots of time with other people who are more fun than you.

To make yourself more attractive to your husband or wife, try to lighten up a bit. Don't take your marital problems so seriously that you lose your sense of humor. Each day look for some opportunity to be playful or silly with your husband or wife. A little good-natured banter goes a long way toward reducing tensions between husbands and wives. Being a bit playful will also perhaps stir in your partner a heightened desire to cooperate and give you more of what you want in relation to your deepest desires and needs.

5. *Get treatment for yourself if you are seriously depressed or anxious or if you think you may have a personality problem.* Although this is not a behavioral technique that you can practice each day, it is critical to your efforts to win cooperation from your spouse that you become as mentally healthy as possible. Sometimes the difficulties that individuals experience in relationships are not as much related to what the spouse is or is not doing as they are to the presence of a personality disorder or even a psychiatric illness in the unhappy partner. For example, states of serious depression can alter the way you perceive events in your life and can make you believe that your marriage is much worse than it actually is. Similarly, the presence of a personality disorder, which means that an individual consistently displays self-defeating behaviors and attitudes like manipulative, hostile, and overly critical ways of relating to others, may make an individual espe-

cially hard to get along with. If you think that you may have a personality disorder and/or a psychiatric illness, it's possible that your spouse is simply reacting to your difficult nature or to your problem. Getting professional help for yourself to overcome personality problems and/or depression and anxiety may help you feel substantially better and may make you a more attractive person to your mate.

This chapter has covered a number of topics that you can think about and use to prepare yourself to begin a process of change in your relationship with your husband or wife. In Chapter 2 you will learn some additional and very important ideas and thinking skills that will improve your psychological health and further increase your chances of improving your relationship with your partner. For now, review the following list of key points to remember and start to use this knowledge for self-improvement. Remember, you want to do all that you can to make yourself attractive to your mate. Becoming an emotionally and behaviorally appealing person is the first critical step in a plan to create positive changes in marriage and to capture your spouse's attention.

KEY POINTS TO REMEMBER

1. Men and women are more alike than different. We are all human beings, with similar hopes, desires, and fears.

2. Any marriage can work if both partners *choose* to do what it takes to make it work.

3. Only you create your self-defeating rage, depression, panic, and dysfunctional behaviors.

4. Negative reactions such as screaming, yelling, pouting, nagging, whining, moping, and blaming will intensify your problems with your partner and may even push him or her toward a new love relationship.

5. When your spouse frustrates you in some personally meaningful area, you experience marital dissatisfaction.

6. When you allow yourself to become emotionally disturbed over one or several areas of dissatisfaction with your spouse, you experience marital disturbance.

7. To stir warm feelings in your husband or wife, speak in a sincere and kind tone of voice, compliment your partner several times per day, be a good sport when your mate frustrates you, and be playful and silly at times.

8. If you are unwilling to display love behaviors toward your partner, you are not in love with him or her.

9. Change yourself into a more attractive and appealing person regardless of whether your husband or wife ever changes.

CHAPTER

2

❧

*How Disturbable
Are You?*

$\mathcal{B}$y transforming yourself into a thoroughly undisturbable person you stand a reasonable chance of increasing emotional pleasure and decreasing emotional pain in your life. An undisturbable nature will also make you a more attractive person to all who know you, including your spouse. In this chapter you will learn how to: (1) think about your thinking; (2) understand the relationship between events, thoughts, emotions, and behaviors; (3) identify and change the ways in which you needlessly disturb yourself over your spouse's uncooperative or irresponsible behaviors and attitudes; and (4) acquire specific psychological skills to cope effectively with your spouse's difficult behaviors. The more you can approach your partner in a reasonable levelheaded manner, the greater the chances of gaining the cooperation you desire.

In the following pages you will learn a great deal about what makes you "tick" emotionally and how you can overcome emotional disturbance toward your spouse when he or she frustrates you. As you read through this chapter, keep in mind that women and men are equally likely and capable of becoming emotionally disturbed about their marital problems. As a species, we humans are very easily aroused emotionally and often in ways that are self-defeating.

THE ABC'S OF EMOTIONAL DISTURBANCE

What follows is based upon the work of Albert Ellis (1994, 1996), one of the most influential and creative psychologists of the twentieth century. Although the following pages provide a concise introduction to Dr. Ellis's work, which he calls Rational Emotive Behavior Therapy (REBT), I encourage you to read a few of the books he and his colleagues have written to augment and deepen your understanding of what you will learn in the following pages. In the suggested reading list at the end of this book you will find some of my favorite REBT selections.

To understand the REBT theory of emotional disturbance, it is critical that you first learn the cornerstone insight or principle upon which REBT theory stands. This principle, which Ellis (1994) attributes to the ancient Greek philosopher Epictetus, says that events in the world do not disturb us as much as the view we take of them. In other words, it is the way you think about or evaluate a bad event that determines your emotional and behavioral responses to that bad event. A statement of this principle in relation to your spouse's uncooperative, obnoxious, or irresponsible behavior would look something like this. *Your partner's difficult and uncooperative behaviors do not enrage, depress, or panic you. You enrage, depress, or panic yourself based on the way you think about or evaluate your partner's bad behavior.*

To be even more specific, imagine four women, each of whom is married to a man who is having an extramarital affair. Do you think all four women would have the same emotional and behavioral reaction to this admittedly bad situation? Very unlikely. Consider the following examples:

1. Emily depressed herself over her husband's affair by thinking, "This is the *worst* possible thing that could ever happen to me. My husband's rejection of me proves that I am a worthless person. I'm going to take an overdose of drugs and kill myself."

2. Rita enraged herself over her husband's bad behavior by thinking, "My husband *must* not treat me in such an unfair way. He and his girlfriend deserve to be killed. I'm going to mow them down with my car."

3. Susan felt appropriately sad, frustrated, hurt, and angry about her husband's affair by thinking, "It's damned unfortunate I married a man who cannot remain faithful. I didn't expect our marriage to turn out this way. I definitely do not want a man who behaves like this. In the morning I'll call my lawyer to start a divorce so I can move on to another more satisfying relationship."

4. Concerning her unfaithful husband, Jane felt worried and upset but she told herself, "I understand that my husband's behavior is part of his midlife crisis and that

his rejection of me has nothing to do with my worth as a person. I'll try to forgive him for being unfaithful and wait it out until he comes to his senses and returns to me."

If you believe that bad events such as a spouse's extramarital affair *always* lead to emotional disturbance, how do you explain the different emotional and behavioral reactions of these four equally betrayed women? The answer lies in the fact that each of these women viewed the husband's extramarital affair (bad behavior) through a different evaluative lens. Two women (Emily and Rita) became severely emotionally disturbed because they used irrational (unhelpful) thinking to process or evaluate the extramarital affairs of their husbands. In short, each of these women took her partner's extramarital affair far too seriously, greatly exaggerated the badness of the situation, and as a result engaged in seriously self-defeating behavior, that is, Emily became suicidal and Rita homicidal.

The other two women, however, reacted with *healthy* sadness, frustration, or worry about the husband's unfaithful behavior, but they did not become emotionally disturbed over the affairs. These women chose to use helpful (rational) thinking to deal with the admittedly bad situation of a husband's extramarital affair. As a result of using a self-helping way of looking at the husband's affair these women then were able to reduce emotional pain and engage in thoughtfully chosen, self-helping courses of action consistent with their goals. These examples clearly illustrate that it is not the difficult events in your life that disturb you as much as the way that you look at your problems.

In his talks and writings, Albert Ellis frequently refers to the ABC's of emotional and behavioral disturbance. In his theory, "A" stands for activating events or adversity in life, "B" stands for beliefs (both rational and irrational), and "C" stands for the emotional and behavioral consequences that occur as reactions to activating events and rational or irrational beliefs. By learning to use the ABC model, you will be better able to sort out, understand, and discard your self-defeating thoughts, emotions, and behaviors and replace them with self-helping thoughts, emotions, and behaviors. Below is a more complete definition of activating events, rational and irrational beliefs, and emotional and behavioral consequences. Under each of the following sections I have included examples as they might pertain to your husband's or wife's difficult behaviors.

A: Activating Events

Activating events are those occurrences in life that are frustrating, provocative, difficult, or painful, or that block you from achieving your goals. Getting stuck in traffic, breaking your leg, being criticized by your mother, or losing your job are examples of activating events. You always have a *choice* about how to think about your activating events.

Your spouse is likely to provide you with plenty of activating events over the course of your marriage. Typical activating events in marriage may include, but are not limited to, your partner's full array of irresponsible or inconsiderate behaviors and attitudes, such as nagging, yelling, name calling, not coming home on time, not doing enough work around the house, drinking too much, messing up the house, having an affair, not giving you enough sex or affection, and so forth. Problems such as these are distinctly unpleasant and frustrating and often not at all under your control. You do, however, control the degree to which you will become emotionally disturbed about your spouse's bad behavior.

B: Beliefs—Rational and Irrational

Picture your belief system as the lens or filter through which you evaluate activating events. Some of the beliefs you have are rational (helpful) and some are irrational (unhelpful). If you use rational beliefs to look at a difficult situation with your spouse, you will become appropriately upset but not emotionally disturbed. If you use irrational beliefs to look at your spouse's bad behaviors and attitudes, you will very likely become emotionally disturbed and engage in self-defeating behaviors. Below are more complete descriptions of rational and irrational beliefs.

Rational beliefs are true in the sense that there is evidence to support them. They are also flexible, tolerant, and strongly preferential in nature. Rational beliefs will help you achieve your goals in life and generally lead you to experience moderate self-helping negative emotions such as sadness, regret, frustration, and concern when your partner frustrates or disappoints you. Examples of rational beliefs about your spouse's inconsiderate actions are thoughts such as the following. "My spouse never has to treat me fairly or considerately though it would be highly preferable if he or she did." "My partner is always a worthwhile person though I may not like his or her bad, irresponsible behaviors." "Though I do not like the way my husband or wife is acting now, I can stand it. There are many worse things that could happen to me."

Irrational beliefs, on the other hand, are not true because there is no evidence to support them. They also have a rigid, grandiose, absolutistic, and demanding nature. Irrational beliefs will often prevent you from achieving your goals and are likely to lead you to experience extremely disturbed, self-defeating, negative emotions such as rage, depression, or severe anxiety and panic. Irrational beliefs are often identified by the presence of unconditional command words such as "should" or "must." For example, "My husband *should* know better than to drink so much." (Oh really?) Or, "My wife *must* do what I want her to." (Good luck!) Or, "My husband is again going out with the boys and leaving me alone, as he *must* not!" (Where is it written in the laws of the universe that you must never be left alone?) Other examples of irrational beliefs about a spouse are, "My husband is a *thoroughly rotten* person who deserves severe punishment for his bad behavior." (Nobody is all bad.) "I *can't stand it* when my wife criticizes me." (You can stand it though you don't like it.) "It's *terrible* when my husband won't talk to me." (Terrible means worse than the worst thing that could ever happen to you.) "If my wife rejects me sexually, I am really a *worthless* person." (Rejection, sexual or otherwise, does not diminish your worth as a person one bit!)

According to REBT theory, you always have irrational and rational beliefs coexisting in your mind (Ellis 1994). People who become emotionally disturbed have turned the volume of their irrational beliefs all the way up so that they are very loud thoughts in the mind and simultaneously have turned the volume of their rational beliefs down to a whisper so they have minimal ability to influence feelings and behavior. Thus, the irrational beliefs will be the main evaluative lens through which the individual views a particular activating event, and by doing so the person will considerably and needlessly disturb himself or herself.

C: Emotional and Behavioral Consequences

The emotional and behavioral consequences that occur in response to any given activating event (situation of frustration or disappointment) can be divided into two categories: (1) healthy, appropriate, negative emotions and (2) unhealthy, inappropriate, negative emotions.

Healthy negative emotions result when you look at a problem with rational (helpful) thoughts. Sadness, regret, concern, frustration, non-damning forms of anger, and mild worry are healthy negative emotions. They are healthy and appropriate because it would not be normal to feel good or to feel nothing when you are faced with a frustrating or disappointing situation (activating event). When you experience healthy negative emotions, you can still think clearly and use such feelings to propel you toward creative solutions to your marital problems or, for that matter, any other difficult life situation.

Unhealthy negative emotions occur when you evaluate a problem with irrational (unhelpful) thoughts. Rage, panic, depression, severe envy, and jealousy are the major inappropriate negative emotions. When you are under the influence of one or several of these emotions, you will be more likely to engage in self-defeating behaviors and will not be able to think clearly. To those around you, you will appear immature, difficult, or extremely insecure, and you will probably do or say something stupid that your spouse will hold against you for a long time. It would seem logical and self-helping, therefore, to try very hard to prevent yourself from ever being overwhelmed by self-sabotaging, inappropriate negative feelings and behaviors.

There is one other point I want you to understand about unhealthy negative emotions. Sometimes your C (e.g., deep depression) can become an A (activating event). In other words, you may become depressed about your depression, angry about your anger, or panicked about your severe anxiety. If this happens, try first to overcome your disturbance about your disturbance and then work on changing or correcting your primary disturbance. For example, Tim became severely depressed over his wife's decision to divorce him. He then thought, "I'm totally bummed out because I *shouldn't* be depressed. Being depressed means I'm a real loser." With some work, Tim was able to overcome his disturbance about his disturbance by thinking, "Where's the evidence that I shouldn't ever become depressed? I'm a human being like everyone else. I can accept myself even with my crummy depression. Now how can I start to work on my primary depression about being rejected and divorced by my wife?"

By now you understand the main point of this section. In a nutshell, your A's (activating events) do not cause your C's (emotional consequences). It is your B's (beliefs) that cause your self-helping or self-defeating emotional and behavioral actions and reactions. The key to being a thoroughly undisturbable person is to be able to identify, dispute, and detonate into oblivion your irrational beliefs. After you have dumped your irrational beliefs in the wastebasket where they belong, you can then train yourself to operate mainly within the framework of helpful rational beliefs or philosophies about life's problems in general and your marital difficulties in particular. Table 2–1 outlines Dr. Ellis's ABC model of emotional disturbance. In the next section you will learn how to dispute and change your self-sabotaging, problematic styles of thinking and irrational beliefs.

PROBLEMATIC STYLES OF THINKING

In this section you will review seven self-defeating types of thinking. Individuals who remain wedded to the following styles of thinking are generally very disturbable people, have great difficulty with problem-solving, and create more emotional disturbance for themselves than is necessary. The good news, however, is that it is possible to change your thinking if you work at it vigorously and consistently. Each of the following sections contains a description of the problematic type of thinking and suggestions to help you challenge and change your unhelpful, self-defeating thoughts into rational, self-helping thoughts.

Table 2–1. Ellis's ABC Model of Emotional Disturbance

A Activating Events	B Beliefs—Rational and Irrational		C Consequences
	Irrational beliefs		Unhealthy negative emotional
All of life's hassles, frustrations, and unfairness	Demand for fairness	→ W	reactions such as rage, depression, panic, and shock; self-sabotaging
	Demand for approval	H →	behaviors such as aggression toward
Situations that prevent you from achieving your goals	Demand for comfort	→ E	others or self-destructive behavior
	Demand for competence	N →	
		F →	
Adversity in life	*Rational beliefs*	R →	Healthy negative emotional reactions
	Preference for fairness	→ U	such as concern, sadness, disappoint-
Your spouse's problematic actions and reactions	Preference for approval	S →	ment, milder anger, and appropriate,
	Preference for comfort	→ T	mature problem-solving behavior
	Preference for competence	R →	
		→ A	
		T →	
		→ E	
		D →	

Adapted from *Reason and Emotion in Psychotherapy, 2nd Ed.* by Albert Ellis, copyright © 1994 by the Institute for Rational-Emotive Therapy. Used by permission of the author and Carol Publishing Co.

Demandingness

Of all the problematic styles of thinking, this is probably the one that most often gets people into serious emotional and behavioral trouble. *Demandingness* occurs when you take your legitimate preferences, desires, hopes, and wishes and transform them into rigid, absolute, intolerant demands. When you think in a demanding way it is as if you are saying to yourself, "I'm the ruler of the universe and I *should* or *must* always get what I want, prefer, or desire." Oh really? Lots of luck! A demanding/commanding type of thinking is often identified by the presence of unconditional demand words such as *should, must,* or *ought* in your self-talk. In some situations the word *need* also betrays a demanding type of thinking, such as, "Because I want you to spend more time with me, I *need* you to spend more time at home." Either way, the presence of unconditional musts, shoulds, oughts, or an unrealistic sense of "need" will generally lead you toward severe self-defeating emotional and behavioral actions and reactions. With respect to your grandiose shoulds, musts, and oughts, you (as ruler of the universe) will often experience "trouble in your kingdom" because your "subjects" continue to act in the way they want to act, in total defiance of your self-proclaimed laws. Thus, you will become enraged, horrified, and deeply disturbed that the world is not working in the way you demand. On the other hand, when you unrealistically transform your preference or desire for love, approval, attention, affection, sex, and other pleasures into *dire* needs, you essentially tell yourself that you will die if you can't get what you want. Ninety-nine percent of what you want you don't need, but if you truly believe you do need love, approval, sex, and the like, you will panic yourself because you will unrealistically and self-defeatingly convince yourself that you can't live without what you want. Does that make sense? The only things you really need for survival are food, water, air, and shelter—that's it! Living without love, approval, companionship, sex, and so forth may be unpleasant, but hardly life-threatening.

Ellis (1994) discovered three basic musts, or forms of demandingness, in humans, each of which has hundreds of variations. The three core demands are: (1) demands on others, (2) demands on yourself, and (3) demands about the conditions of your life. Demands on others often involve the idea that others *must* treat you fairly and considerately and if they don't they are totally rotten beasts who deserve severe and eternal punishment and damnation. Conversely, demands on yourself generally involve rigid beliefs that you *must* have the approval of important people in your life or that you *must* perform perfectly and competently all the time. Otherwise, either way (that is, without approval from others or perfect performance on your part), you are a worthless person. Finally, demands about life conditions have to do with the absolute conviction that you *must* always be comfortable, get what you want without effort, or that you *must not* get what you don't want because that would make you uncomfortable (as you *must* not be). All these areas of demandingness contain your legitimate preferences for (1) fair and considerate treatment by others, (2) approval from others, (3) outstanding performance by you and your spouse, and (4) comfort and pleasure in life. Hold on to your strong legitimate preferences, values, desires, and goals but tear up and discard your irrational demands. Life often doesn't work the way you want it to. Like it or not, that's the way it is. If you work vigorously to maintain a strongly preferential non-demanding philosophy about life, you will be less likely to become emotionally disturbed because you will be better equipped to accept, tolerate, and cope with life's hassles and your own and your spouse's fallible nature.

To get rid of your irrational demands, first identify them by looking for the unconditional shoulds, have to's, musts, oughts, and needs in your self-talk. Then use the following three questions and answers to challenge, dispute, and discard your demandingness.

- *Question 1*: Where is the evidence that I must get what I want, or that others must treat me fairly?
- *Answer*: There is no evidence that others should or must treat me fairly or that I must get what I want, though it would be highly preferable if others did treat me fairly or if I were able to get what I want out of life and my marriage.

- *Question 2*: Does it make sense that I must get what I want?
- *Answer*: It makes no sense whatsoever. In fact, it is downright illogical to conclude that I must get what I want.

- *Question 3*: Does thinking in a demanding way help me to achieve my goals?

- *Answer:* No. Thinking in a demanding way only makes me emotionally disturbed when the world does not work in the way I demand. I then begin to say and do stupid things that prevent me from achieving my goals and that I later regret.

Again, if you work at it you can change your irrational, unhealthy demands back to rational, healthy, flexible preferences and in this way take an important step toward being a thoroughly undisturbable person. Let's now move on to consider other types of unhealthy thinking.

Catastrophizing

Catastrophizing occurs when you exaggerate the badness of an event or situation or your spouse's inconsiderate and irresponsible behaviors. Catastrophizing seems to be a natural human tendency as evidenced by the fact that most people define as holy horrors many things that are in fact only unfortunate, discomforting, or inconvenient events/situations. You can usually identify your catastrophizing by the presence of words like horrible, terrible, and awful in your self-talk. When you tell yourself that a given situation or your spouse's bad behavior is horrible, terrible, or awful, you are really saying that the bad behavior or situation is worse than the worst thing that could ever happen to you (Ellis and Dryden 1997). With this definition in mind, does it make any sense at all to describe your spouse's undesirable behaviors and attitudes as horrible or terrible? Is your husband's or wife's bad or irresponsible behavior the worst thing that could ever happen to you, let alone worse than that?

To combat your tendency to catastrophize, stop using the words *horrible, terrible,* and *awful.* Instead substitute the words *unfortunate* or *inconvenient.* It's only unfortunate or inconvenient or discomforting when your husband or wife gets going with those behaviors or attitudes over which you make yourself feel "nuts." Also try to imagine the worst thing that could ever happen to you, like being run over by a train or learning that you have an aggressive, inoperable cancer that will kill you in three months. Now ask yourself, "Is my husband's or wife's bad behavior, such as an affair, substance abuse, chronically angry mood, laziness, or sloppiness, as bad as that or anything else I might decide would be the worst thing that could ever happen to me?" If your answer is yes, you are still catastrophizing and will need to work vigorously to put your marital problems in a more realistic, less catastrophic perspective. As long as you keep catastrophizing, you will be exaggerating the badness of your problems and will likely be overwhelmed or flooded with inappropriate emotions such as rage, panic, or depression.

To develop the capacity to view the larger picture, review the following personal catastrophe scale (Table 2–2).

Trashing Others or Yourself

Trashing a person (or yourself) means that you globally rate or evaluate someone as totally bad, wicked, or evil because that person has treated you in some unfair, abusive, or inconsiderate manner, and for that reason he or she deserves

Table 2-2. Personal Catastrophe Scale

---

10 = Horrible-Terrible-Awful = worse than the worst thing that could ever happen to me.

9 to 1 = Unfortunate events or circumstances.

Horrible	→	10 - Atom bomb destroys my state—everyone dies.
The worst	→	9 - My whole family dies.
		8 - Car accident leaves me paralyzed.
		7 - My spouse divorces me.
		6 - My spouse has an affair.
		5 - I lose my job.
		4 - My spouse yells at me.
		3 - The cleaner ruins my shirt.
		2 - The house is messy.
		1 - I break a nail.

Adapted from *Winning Cooperation from Your Child!: A Comprehensive Method to Stop Defiant and Aggressive Behavior in Children* by Kenneth Wenning, copyright © 1996.

severe condemnation and eternal excruciating punishment in hell. You can detect your trashing tendencies by the presence of common rude epithets such as, "He is a total loser, crumb, or scum bag," or even more degrading terms such as bitch, asshole, or total shit. The presence of self-talk like this means that you have taken a complex fallible human being and reduced that person to the lowly status of an evil single body part, bodily product, or an all-bad person. When you allow yourself to perceive another person or your spouse in this way, you first lose all empathy for that person and then become obsessively and self-defeatingly focused on revenge as a way of delivering the punishment you irrationally believe your husband or wife deserves. Does this type of thinking seem healthy or mature to you? Does it make any kind of sense at all?

Trashing yourself involves the same psychological process, only it is aimed at you. When you trash yourself, you globally rate yourself as a failure, a loser, or a worthless person because you either failed to function perfectly or failed to receive approval from an important person such as your spouse. Your tendency to globally put yourself down can be detected in labels like "loser," "failure," "no hoper," "worthless," and so forth, which you self-defeatingly apply to yourself. And, after you have trashed yourself in this way, you then further conclude that you probably are undeserving of anything good in life and that your spouse's inconsiderate, rude, or inappropriate behaviors are probably exactly what you do deserve because a "loser" like you should suffer for a long, long time. Does this type of thinking seem healthy or make sense to you? I hope not.

To overcome your tendency to trash or globally devalue your spouse (or yourself), separate your husband's or wife's bad behavior from his or her worth as a person. Your partner may be displaying rude and obnoxious behavior, but that does not mean that he or she is worthless or all bad. Your spouse is always and unconditionally a worthwhile human being who is fallible. Rate your partner's behaviors and attitudes as good or bad but not his or her worth as a person. If you think this way, you will be better able to stay focused on the problems you want fixed and you will not get caught up in self-defeating efforts to torture or punish your "evil" mate.

You can also apply such thinking toward yourself. That is, you too are always and unconditionally a worthwhile person, whether or not you receive approval from others or perform perfectly. And, keep in mind that just as disapproval from others or poor performance in a task or role does not decrease your worth as a person, excellent performance or approval from others does not increase your worth either. If you elevate your own or your spouse's worth based on good deeds, you will at times end up worshiping yourself or your spouse, which simply sets you up for a depressive "crash" when your own or your partner's fallibility surfaces again. So do not trash or worship yourself or your spouse. Instead accept yourself and others fully and unconditionally, that is, with all the faults that make us human. You will be a happier and less disturbable person if you do.

I-Can't-Stand-It-Itis

I-can't-stand-it-itis (low frustration tolerance) (Dryden and DiGiuseppe 1990) reflects your tendency to unrealistically view many common, inconvenient, uncomfortable, or annoying situations as unbearable (i.e., life-threatening)—so bad you will die if the bad situation or your spouse's obnoxious behavior continues. When you say to yourself, "I can't bear it" or "I can't stand it" when your husband or wife is inconsiderate or thoughtless, you are having an attack of "I-can't-stand-it-itis," which is based upon a philosophy of low frustration tolerance (LFT).

Low frustration tolerance usually surfaces in one of two ways. One variation is the irrational (unhelpful) belief that you *must* always get what you want easily and without effort, and if you don't get what you want easily you "can't stand it."

The other type of LFT is based on the totally irrational belief that the world or your spouse *must* never do or say something you don't want, or that would make you feel uncomfortable or annoyed, such as rude, difficult, irresponsible behavior or asking you to work, because such inconveniences would be unbearable. Does this make sense to you? Do you think that a philosophy of LFT will help you solve problems with your spouse? Probably not.

There are two psychological antidotes to LFT (I-can't-stand-it-itis): (1) Dispute and discard your irrational demand for your life to be easy and for the world to work in just the way you want it to. For example, ask yourself, "Does it make any sense at all that just because I want my life to be easy it must be?" "Where is the evidence that I can't bear feelings of discomfort or difficult/frustrating situations with my spouse? I haven't died from this situation so far, nor have I gone blind or lost my hair." (2) Vigorously work at developing a lifelong philosophy of high frustration tolerance (HFT), which is based upon the idea that you can literally bear or stand anything until you do die! In difficult situations with your spouse tell yourself, "I don't like it but I *can* stand it."

Black/White Thinking

Black/white thinking is a self-defeating, overgeneralized, and rigid way of looking at situations, problems, or events. Such thinking is characterized by sharp either/or distinctions between good and bad or right and wrong, with no ability to consider all the in-between perspectives or options.

You can notice black/white thinking in your self-talk in thoughts like, "My point of view is absolutely right and my spouse's point of view is absolutely wrong." Or, "There is only one right way to solve this problem with my spouse: *my way!* No other solution is possible or acceptable." Or, "What I want and need is good and what my spouse wants or needs is bad." Sharp distinctions between right and wrong or good and bad will lead others to view you as an extremely rigid person who has little or no ability to compromise or be flexible in problem solving with your spouse. Problem solving in marriage usually requires creative, open, and flexible thinking that goes far beyond simple reductionistic, black/white distinctions of good and bad or right and wrong.

To overcome your black/white thinking ask yourself, "Is my point of view on my problems really the only possible point of view about what is good, bad, right, or wrong?" "Why are my desires, preferences, and needs always defined as good or right and those of others defined as bad or wrong? Do I think that I'm the only person on this planet whose point of view matters?" And you can tell yourself the following, "Mostly things in life are relatively good or bad or relatively right or wrong. Between all good (right) and all bad (wrong) there are many shades of gray that represent *opportunities* for me to see things differently and to create many possible solutions with my partner. The solutions or perspectives that fall between sharp good/bad or right/wrong distinctions may not exactly be to my liking, but I can learn to compromise, be flexible, and factor my spouse's desires and needs into the final solution to our problems *if I really want to solve them.*"

Tunnel Vision

Tunnel vision is a type of thinking characterized by an over-developed focus on half the picture when trying to problem solve or sustain a relationship with your husband or wife. If you suffer from tunnel vision, you selectively focus on some of your spouse's qualities and at the same time choose to ignore his or her other qualities. For example, you may become selectively focused on your spouse's negative qualities, such as obnoxious and irresponsible behaviors, and at the same time you may ignore strengths and positive qualities, such as pleasing and responsible behaviors. When tunnel vision leads you to be overly focused on your partner's negative qualities, you then begin to define your spouse's entire being in terms of these negative qualities. Do you think that your spouse will want to spend time with you or try to respond to your desires if you view him or her as a person only with negative qualities? Probably not!

Tunnel vision can also show up in exactly the opposite form. In some cases of tunnel vision individuals see only the positive qualities of the spouse and completely ignore the negatives. For example, a wife may view her husband as always a wonderful person even though he periodically drinks to excess, leaves home for days at a time, and has a temper problem. With this type of tunnel vision a spouse will likely never give up or modify his bad behaviors. Why should he? He's got a great thing going. No matter what he does that is irresponsible or obnoxious, his wife doesn't see it. Why change?

To overcome your tunnel vision you can use a simple "double column technique" to expand your view of your spouse. The technique involves listing on a piece of paper your partner's positive qualities on one side of the page and negative qualities on the other side. Remember, as a human being, even the most wonderful person in the world has negative qualities and the most obnoxious, irresponsible person in the world has positive qualities. If you work at it you can overcome your tunnel vision and by doing so gain a more realistic view of your spouse.

Always/Never Thinking

Always/never thinking is a type of overgeneralization in which one or several bad events are used as the basis for a sweeping evaluation of your spouse's behavior or as the basis for predicting the course of the rest of your life. Always/never thinking is also a form of crazy logic. For example, Jane might be legitimately frustrated over an episodically inattentive husband. Out of desperation, however, she might then fall into always/never thinking and make a self-defeating comment like, "You *never* pay any attention to me." Such a statement is very likely untrue. In this case Jane might also say something like, "You *always* pay attention to what you want. I *never* get what I want." Again, such statements are probably inaccurate.

Always/never thinking can also show up in your tendency to trash the entire rest of your life based on past or current misfortunes. For example, George, who has just been divorced by his wife might wrongly and self-defeatingly conclude, "Now that my wife has left me I'm *never* going to find another woman. I'm *always* going to be alone and miserable for the rest of my life, while my ex-wife will *always* be happy for the rest of hers." This is truly nutty logic because none of us has a crystal ball with which to predict the future. Always/ never thinking when used in relation to the future is like saying, "Because something bad is happening to me now it's always going to be this way." Or, "Because I've lost something that was truly delicious and pleasurable I'll never have such pleasures again." If you really believe that you can predict the future in this way, you really are a bit crazy.

To overcome your always/never thinking you need to censor your use of the words always and never. That is, each time you notice yourself using these words, actively block their verbalization and privately ask yourself, "Is 'always' really an accurate term here?" Or, "Is 'never' really the way I want to conceptualize this problem?" If you're honest with yourself you will quickly see that rarely in life are things totally one way or another. Even if your spouse is displaying many obnoxious or irresponsible behaviors it is likely that once in a while he or she comes through for you, pays attention to you, and meets your needs in some way. With respect to your use of always/ never thinking in relation to your future, all you have to do is look at friends or colleagues who have experienced misfortune but who have been able to recover enjoyable, pleasurable lives. In other words, just look around you and you'll see that rarely does it happen that we are plagued by complete misfortune for an entire lifetime. If you begin to think in these self-helping ways, you will be able to overcome your always/never thinking.

BECOMING AN UNDISTURBABLE PERSON

By now you have started to learn that you are in control of your thoughts, feelings, and behaviors and that you can become a thoroughly undisturbable person if you work at it vigorously, because *no one but you makes you disturbed*. So work to undisturb yourself over your spouse's various obnoxious, irresponsible, and childish behaviors. (Hopefully by now your partner is also undisturbing himself or herself over your difficult and nutty behaviors and attitudes.) In other words, marital happiness rests in large measure upon you and your spouse not taking each other's inconsiderate and irresponsible behaviors so seriously that you each become emotionally disturbed.

Becoming an undisturbable person does not mean that you train yourself to feel nothing in the face of difficult situations with your spouse. You would not be human if you felt nothing in trying or challenging moments. Instead I encourage you to strongly feel all the self-helping, appropriate negative emotions such as regret, concern, mild worry, and mild to moderate non-damning anger and frustration. These healthy negative emotions will not cloud your judgment and can be used as the engine that drives you toward long-lasting solutions to your marital problems or toward a decision to end a chronically unsatisfying relationship with your husband or wife.

To strengthen your ability to become an undisturbable person, review Table 2–3 (Personal Disturbability Scale) and estimate the degree to which you allow yourself to become self-defeatingly agitated and disturbed. Next practice the following coping statements one to two times per day.

Table 2–3. Personal Disturbability Scale—How Disturbable Are You?

Emotional Description		Belief Description
You are extremely reactive to problems in life. You quickly fly off the handle when frustrated and spew rage, panic, depression, panic easily. Much of the time you are a real basket case.	IRRATIONAL ___	You devoutly believe that your self-defeating emotions of rage, panic, depression, shock are caused by other people or bad situations. You believe that you have no responsibility for your dysfunctional emotional reactions.
You show good emotional control when frustrated yet remain capable of feeling healthy negative emotions such as sadness, disappointment, regret, non-damning anger.	RATIONAL ___	You understand that bad events in the world do not disturb you as much as the way you look at or evaluate bad events. You believe that you are personally responsible for your self-defeating emotional and behavioral reactions.
You are so emotionally detached from the world that your house could burn down around you and you would not notice or react.	IRRATIONAL	What you believe is not clear because you live in a world of private thought. You appear to value a very rigid boundary between you and the external world. One of your beliefs might be a demand to see and feel nothing.

By recognizing the degree to which you are disturbable and working vigorously to change your thinking and your self-talk, you will be able to tolerate many difficult situations with your spouse and gain greater control over your emotional destiny.

You should know that I try very hard to practice what I preach. During the course of my marriage, I have many times started to make myself emotionally disturbed over some area of dissatisfaction with my wife. At these moments of self-induced disturbance I have vigorously conducted therapy on myself using the same philosophies, techniques, and coping statements described in this chapter. By doing so I have usually been able to overcome my self-defeating, unhealthy, negative emotions quite rapidly and, as a result, I have been much more successful at solving my marital problems or gracefully accepting things I cannot change. I will also share with you that some of the therapy I have done and continue to do on myself has started to rub off on my wife so that now she is less disturbed about her dissatisfactions with me. Our marriage has become more pleasurable because we do not take our respective marital dissatisfactions so seriously that either of us becomes horrified, enraged, panicked, or depressed when frustrated—most of the time!

Coping Statements to Promote Psychological Strength

1. I accept that I am solely responsible for my emotional and behavioral reactions toward my spouse. Nobody but me makes me emotionally disturbed.

2. In any difficult or conflictual situation with my spouse I always have a choice about how to think and feel about the problem.

3. Although I strongly wish that my spouse would behave in less obnoxious and more responsible ways, there is no law of the universe that says he or she has to do anything I want.

4. Although I do not like my spouse's bad behaviors, he or she is a fallible human being and always a worthwhile person.

5. I can handle it when I don't get what I want from my partner or when my partner does or says something that I don't want. Either way I'll live.

6. Dealing with my spouse's difficult and irresponsible behaviors is not the worst thing that could happen to me. In fact, there are many things that could happen to me that would be far worse than my current marital problems.

7. If I am getting overly angry at my spouse, it means I am transforming my legitimate preferences and desires into rigid, intolerant, God-like demands for good behavior from my spouse.

8. If I am getting overly angry, it means that I have appointed myself ruler of the universe and that I believe I absolutely must, should, or ought to get what I want. My outburst of rage toward my spouse is nothing more

than an infantile temper tantrum because I can't get what I irrationally believe I must have.

9. When I make mistakes toward my spouse I will forgive myself because I am a fallible human being.

10. I will not put myself down when I make mistakes. Instead, I will try to learn from my mistakes to improve myself and to improve my relationship with my husband or wife.

11. I will likely work out more solutions with my partner if my thinking is open, tolerant, preferential, and flexible.

12. I will likely find more solutions to my marital problems if I avoid black/white thinking, always/never thinking, catastrophizing, trashing myself or my spouse, tunnel vision, and I-can't-stand-it-itis.

13. I will definitely be more attractive to my spouse if I work at displaying kindness, openness, honesty, tolerance, patience, and playfulness as we struggle to work out our marital difficulties.

14. When my *preferences* are frustrated, I will feel healthy negative emotions such as sadness, concern, moderate anger, disappointment, and so forth. When my *demands* are frustrated, I will feel unhealthy negative emotions such as rage, shock, horror, deep depression, or panic.

✎

KEY POINTS TO REMEMBER

1. Bad events in life do not disturb you as much as the way you think about or evaluate bad events.

2. Irrational beliefs are generally rigid, demanding, intolerant, absolute, and grandiose in nature.

3. Irrational beliefs lead to self-defeating negative emotions such as rage, depression, panic, shock, and infantile behavior—screaming, threatening, stomping out of the house, moping, and so forth.

4. Rational beliefs are flexible, tolerant, preferential, and nondemanding.

5. Rational beliefs lead to self-helping negative emotions such as concern, non-damning anger, disappointment, sadness, and mature problem-solving behavior.

6. You do not have the power to change your spouse. You do have the power to change your behavior and your thinking if you work at it vigorously.

Attractive
Communication
Skills

$\mathcal{T}$he way you communicate with your spouse will either help or hinder your efforts to solve your marital problems. The goal of this chapter is to teach you eight attractive communication skills that will likely make it easier for you and your partner to understand each other's point of view, find common ground, and solve problems. You will also learn four techniques to stop conflicts with your husband or wife from escalating into major "blow outs." To get started, let's quickly review a few key ideas about communication and the eight unattractive cardinal communication sins.

SOME THOUGHTS
ABOUT COMMUNICATION

Unlike all other life forms on our planet, humans have the unique gift of language, which allows us to verbally communicate with each other at a level far beyond the grunts and snorts of less evolved animals. What this means is that you can take the contents of your mind, such as ideas, perceptions, feelings, complaints, hopes, dreams, sorrows, memories, and so forth, convert them into audible sound patterns (spoken language), and transmit them through the air to your spouse for consideration. After receiving your message, your partner is then able to formulate a response and, by the same process, transmit reactions back to you for your consideration, and so forth. This is a truly remarkable and uniquely human capacity. And, language gives you and your spouse the power to *harmlessly* share any idea, complaint, or feeling you have with each other.

In our current "politically correct" era a very crazy idea has gained wide acceptance. It is an idea that is so utterly preposterous and irrational it is hard to believe that it is devoutly held by millions of humans. What I am referring to is the notion that ideas and spoken words can harm or hurt people. Despite overwhelming evidence to the contrary, many men and women actually believe they have the power to wound people if they openly and honestly share thoughts, feelings, or complaints that may be hard for others to hear. To set the record straight, therefore, let me forcefully say: *your ideas and spoken words do not have the power to harm anyone.* Individuals who become upset or disturbed over your ideas and words are psychologically weak and immature. Such people are weak because they cling to irrational beliefs about what others *must* or *must not* say and/ or what they *can* or *cannot* stand to hear, or they wrongly believe that mean words dimish personal worth. By holding rigidly to such beliefs, they horrify, depress, or enrage themselves about your hard-to-hear but harmless ideas and words.

The other side of this coin is that no one can ever hurt, wound, or insult you unless you allow them to. If you demand that others not tell you hard-to-hear things or insist that you can't stand it when a rude remark comes your way, you will create self-defeating emotional disturbance in yourself because, like it or not, other people, including your spouse, will at times tell you things you do not want to hear.

To prove that ideas and words can do absolutely no harm to anyone, imagine that your spouse says that he or she is embarrassed by the way you dress, or is unhappy with your current lovemaking methods, or becomes angry with you and begins hurling insults such as "You rotten bastard!" or "I hope you rot in hell!" If any of these situations were to occur, it would definitely be frustrating and unpleasant, but would you be damaged in any way? Would your worth as a person be diminished at all? The answer to both questions is absolutely not. No part of you would be damaged or devalued unless you have nutty beliefs that would lead you to wrongly believe that your worth as a person had been taken away or that you were somehow harmed by unpleasant words. Psychologically healthy individuals allow all kinds of unpleasant, rude, inconsiderate, and insensitive words to bounce off them because they know words and ideas do not have the power to do any harm at all unless they allow them to!

I am not saying that you should disregard the message in your partner's criticism. I am in fact saying quite the opposite. Be very receptive to your spouse's concerns, frustrations, dissatisfactions, and complaints. But always remember that your partner's hard-to-hear words and ideas neither pose threats to your personal safety nor diminish your worth as a person.

There is one exception to the points I have just made. Children are by nature cognitively immature, dependent, and gullible. That is, they are easily influenced by the adults upon whom they depend for care, protection, and truthful information. Thus, they tend to believe what trusted adults say to them. Mean words aimed at a child will not harm him or her physically, but they may create psychological harm by instilling in the child any number of irrational beliefs, including irrational beliefs about human worth. For example, a child may wrongly learn to believe that he or she is a worthless person without the approval of others.

Having made the point that words and ideas cannot harm others (except possibly children), I want you to understand that I do not advocate the use of rude, blunt, or abusive talk to others. In other words, now that you know that your ideas and words cannot harm others, I do not want you to use this knowledge as a license to blast others with your words and then blame them when they horrify and disturb themselves over your verbal attacks. I am very much an advocate of using sensitivity, tact, and polite talk when you communicate with other people or your spouse. With these thoughts in mind, let's now move on to consider the eight cardinal communication sins.

CARDINAL COMMUNICATION SINS

Humans seem to have a strong propensity for acting in self-defeating ways even when they are aware that they are displaying foolish, immature, and self-sabotaging behaviors such as tirades of anger or moping. The following section reviews eight of the most dysfunctional forms of communication that will almost certainly push your mate away from you and make him or her less interested in solving problems (Table 3–1). If you engage in any of the following self-defeating, unattractive communication behaviors, actively work with yourself to stop these behaviors and instead practice the self-helping, attractive communication behaviors you will learn in the last part of this chapter.

Threats and Ultimatums

Threats and ultimatums represent desperate cornering tactics that are designed to force your partner to give you what you want. When cornered, most humans either fight back with a vengeance or become even more determined to defy the person who is throwing out threats and ultimatums. Also, many individuals rarely follow through on their threats and ultimatums, which will likely strengthen in the person being threat-

---

Table 3–1. Cardinal Communication Sins

1. Threats and ultimatums
2. Dredging up the past
3. Personal attacks
4. Minimizing partner's point of view
5. Guilt trips
6. Changing the topic
7. Emotional abandonment
8. Zapping

---

ened the conviction that he or she does not have to take the spouse's threats and ultimatums seriously.

Dredging Up the Past

When one is trying to solve a current problem, it rarely helps to bring up past problems. When you *dredge up old problems*, you are basically trying to indict your spouse for past crimes in an effort to "guilt trip" him or her into giving you what you want now. Most of the time this tactic leads to an increase of arguing, frustration, and a sense of despair as you and your partner feel buried beneath a mountain of unresolved issues and accusations.

Here I will offer a quick piece of advice. Place a "statute of limitations" on your husband's or wife's bad, irresponsible behaviors. Except in the case of newly discovered troubles, don't bring up any problem that is more than two weeks old. Keep your sights focused on the present and the future. You cannot change the past, but you can alter the future if you work at it.

Personal Attacks

When you give in to your urge to *personally attack* your spouse with curses or words like *loser, failure*, or *scum bag*, you are going for the psychological jugular. At this point you are aggressively trying to wound, humiliate, or trash your spouse so that he or she will feel hurt the way you hurt or so that you will briefly have a self-righteous feeling of superiority over that "rotten" spouse of yours. Attacking your spouse in this way is dirty fighting. It leads you nowhere and it makes you look bad—like you can't handle difficult situations. Give it up!

Minimizing or Discounting Your Partner's Point of View

When you *minimize or discount your spouse's point of view*, you essentially convey the following message: "You really don't mean what you are saying." Or, "Your point of view couldn't possibly be as important as my point of view." How do you feel when others dismiss your point of view? If you're like most people you probably get pretty angry. Humans generally want their ideas to be taken seriously and given due consideration.

Guilt Trips

Laying a *guilt trip* on your spouse to win cooperation from him or her is one of the most self-defeating forms of manipulation you can engage in. Why? Because guilt-motivated behaviors displayed by your spouse are produced by your coercion, not by your husband's or wife's genuine desire to help you, which is what you really want. Also, if you do succeed in making your spouse feel guilty, it will also likely generate feelings of resentment in him or her because most people know when they are being manipulated with or by guilt. Ultimately the guilt trips you dish out and the guilt-motivated behavior they elicit from your partner will leave each of you feeling unsatisfied, unfulfilled, and resentful.

Changing the Topic

In order to resolve conflicts with your spouse you need to be able to vigorously stick to the topic. If you and your partner frequently *change the topic* by introducing new issues or past problems, you will end up in a tangle of unresolved tension points and conflicts. If you find that you and your spouse are wandering off the main point, stop the discussion and get back to the original problem you want to solve. After you solve one problem, move on to the next one.

Emotional Abandonment

Emotional abandonment means that in the midst of trying to solve a problem with your mate you become so frustrated that you withdraw emotionally from your spouse. You may still be in the room sitting there listening to him or her, but in your mind you have "left the building." Your partner can sense this by the vacant glassy stare in your eyes that betrays your contempt for and frustration with his or her point of view. Emotional abandonment is also signaled by your eye-rolling behavior and heavy sighs. Acting in this way will get you nowhere fast in your efforts to solve your problems with your partner. No matter how hard it is, try to hang in there with respect, interest, and concern for your partner's point of view.

Zapping

All those nasty little "zingers" or insults that you shoot at your partner constitute *zapping* behavior. Zapping reflects your sarcastic, maladaptive efforts to use "one-liners" to prove a point or to put your husband or wife down. Zapping will usually elicit defensive counterattacks from your spouse and will most likely result in a counterproductive sparring match if not an outright argument.

If you engage in any or all of these self-defeating communication-destroying behaviors, you will undermine your efforts to work out a more satisfying relationship with your partner. Now that you have worked on these issues let's move on to consider ways to improve or enhance communication, sharing, and understanding between you and your spouse. Keep in mind that men and women are *equally* capable of learning and using all the following attractive communication behaviors if they choose to.

THE BASICS OF CLEAN, ATTRACTIVE COMMUNICATION BEHAVIORS

In this section you will learn eight communication behaviors that will increase your chances of working out problems with your spouse and will make you a more popular and attractive person to others. You can start practicing all the following techniques right away with your spouse (Table 3–2). Be sure to keep using all these attractive communication behaviors even if it seems that your partner is not changing at all. It is more likely than not that your husband or wife has started to notice the positive changes you're making.

Table 3–2. Attractive Communication Behaviors

1. Maintain interest in spouse's point of view
2. Actively listen to spouse
3. Use "I" statements
4. Ask clarifying questions
5. Paraphrase partner's point of view
6. Give constructive feedback to spouse
7. Be clear, direct, to the point
8. Maintain empathy for mate's point of view

1. Maintain an attitude of interest and concern about your spouse's point of view. Even if you are angry at your spouse, it is critical that the overall tone of your approach to problem solving be positive. You can create a positive problem-solving atmosphere by first working to undisturb yourself over the particular problem (activating event) you wish to solve, and then mustering feelings of concern (as opposed to rage), hopefulness (as opposed to despair), and sincerity (as opposed to sarcasm) to approach your partner in a sane, nondefensive manner. Whether your spouse will be able to respond to you is another question. If he or she does not respond, do not enrage or horrify yourself over your partner's nonresponsive behavior. Just keep plugging away with a sane, reasonable approach until you hit the point where you feel it is not worth it to try anymore. You will know when you have hit your critical limit for what you can take from your spouse.

2. Actively listen to your spouse's point of view. The skill of active listening is one of the most valuable communication skills you can learn. Active listening means blocking your urge to talk and listening intensely to what your partner is trying to tell you. Active listening allows you to collect important information from your spouse that you can use to change yourself or to propose reasonable solutions to your marital problems. It is also important that you maintain eye contact while you are listening to your spouse so that he or she knows you are paying attention. When you actively listen in a non-defensive manner to your spouse's point of view, he or she will feel responded to and heard. If your partner believes that you have heard and understood this point of view, it may make it possible for him or her to listen to your point of view.

It seems that psychologically healthy men and women are able to maintain a nice balance between talking and listening in their relationships. If you are an overly talkative person, that is, the nonstop talker type, you will find it hard to block your urge to talk and let your spouse's ideas enter your mind. In my years of counseling couples, some of the toughest cases I've had involved individuals who would not stop talking. These individuals really did not want to change themselves at all. Instead they invested a great deal of energy in spewing out their point of view, that is, their demands on others and the world. In my opinion, these individuals were avoiding change in themselves in favor of changing the world and everyone in it. (Good luck to them!) Needless to say, men and women who cannot listen to others often end up as some of the most frustrated and miserable people around because they push others away with a continual torrent of their ideas and words.

3. *Emphasize the use of the word "I."* "I" statements will help you get your partner's attention and will likely reduce the

arguing, defensiveness, and counterattacks that usually flow from blame-oriented "you" statements. "I" statements will also help your partner understand exactly how you think and feel about some problem or some aspect of his or her irresponsible or obnoxious behavior and what you will or will not tolerate. If you make "you" statements (e.g., "You sure do take care of yourself!" "You always pay attention to your needs!" "You make sure you get what you want!" "You always do things your way!" "You never listen/respond/work!"), you very likely blame, blame, blame your partner. Do you think your partner wants to listen to all your "you" statements and accusations?

Examples of productive "I" statements are as follows: "I think we have a problem that I would like to discuss with you." "I feel worried (concerned, angry, frustrated, sad, disappointed) about the way you are treating me." "You are not a bad person, but I don't like your behavior right now." "I hope we can work out a solution to our problems." "I don't think I can stay in this relationship if we are not able to solve our problems." "I hope you will think about what I have said and make some changes in your behavior." If you incorporate "I" statements into your repertoire of communication skills, your spouse will know exactly where you stand on issues and what your limits are, and you will appear confident and self-assured.

4. *Ask clarifying questions.* When you are talking to your spouse about a problem, it is important not to let any statement or response remain vague or ambiguous. Vague statements are often used as "loopholes" by your spouse to avoid

change or they can become a source of later conflict because you and your partner really did not understand what you were agreeing to. For example, Julia might ask her husband Don if he would consider spending more time at home to be with her and the children. Don's response might be something like, "I'll try my best to be home more." If Julia lets a comment like this go without asking Don what he means, she and Don have not really solved the problem or reached an understanding of what is and is not possible with respect to Don's spending more time at home. To clarify, Julia could say something like, "Don, I'm not sure I understand what you mean when you say you will try your best to be home more. Can you say a little more about what you were thinking to help me understand?"

Examples of clarifying questions are: "What do you mean?" "I don't understand your point. Can you say a little more?" "I think I need a little more information to help me understand your point of view." "Do you mean X, Y, or Z?" "I think I'm beginning to get your point, but tell me in a nutshell what you really want (or don't want) from me."

5. *Paraphrase your partner's point of view.* To be doubly sure that you and your partner do understand each other, it is also important periodically to paraphrase your spouse's main points and look for confirmation that you've got it right. For example, after further discussion and clarification with Don, Julia should paraphrase his response to her request that he spend more time at home. She might say something like, "So what you are saying is that for the next month you have to work overtime on a high-priority project. This will make it hard for

you to be home in the evening on school nights, but you're willing to give up your golf game on Sundays to spend more time with us. Is that right?" Julia then looks for Don to confirm or deny the accuracy of her summary of his position on spending more time at home.

Examples of phrases to start paraphrasing are:

"Let me see if I've got this straight. You're saying. . . ."
"So your main point is. . . ."
"Let me repeat what I think you are saying."

6. *Give your husband or wife feedback when talking.* No one likes to talk to an unresponsive person. Think about it. When you talk to your husband or wife you look for all kinds of verbal and nonverbal feedback that gives you some idea as to whether you have been heard, understood, or misunderstood. When your partner is talking to you, maintain eye contact and verbally acknowledge his or her points with short phrases like, "I see," "O.K.," "I understand," "All right," or "I hear what you are saying," and so forth. You can also periodically praise your partner for sharing a point of view, even if you disagree with it. For example, a husband might say to his wife, "Jane, I don't agree with what you are saying but I'm pleased that you have expressed your point of view. I think we need to talk some more to work out a compromise."

7. *Be clear, to the point, and direct.* In a polite and assertive (not aggressive) manner, state your point of view succinctly. Try not to beat around the bush or bring in all kinds of irrelevant details that will confuse and confound your effort to

problem-solve with your spouse. Try to state your basic position on a problem in 50 words or less. For example, Carla might say to her husband, "Marco, I think that we have been spending too much money lately. I'd like to talk to you about setting up a budget to curtail some of my spending and some of yours." If Marco agrees, he and Carla can then have further discussion about the details of a budget. If he disagrees, he and Carla then need to address their disagreement about whether a budget is needed. Either way Carla and Marco will stand a better chance of working things out if they keep their ideas focused, to the point, and brief.

8. *Maintain a sense of empathy for your partner's point of view.* Empathy for others is the skill of being able to put yourself in another person's shoes. In other words, to develop empathy for another person try as best you can to understand and feel things the way the other person does. There are several ways you can stretch your empathy for your spouse's point of view. First, try to remember that your spouse feels as strongly and passionately about his or her wants, needs, and desires as you do about yours. And, remember also that you are not the only one with frustration that stems from unfulfilled desires. Next, imagine that you are on a debate team and have been assigned the task of arguing *in favor* of your spouse's point of view, even if you are vehemently opposed to it. For example, you could muster arguments to support the following hypothetical positions held by your spouse: (1) why we can't afford a vacation this year; (2) why I shouldn't do any work around the house; (3) why you should give me more support and under-

standing; (4) why we don't need a budget to run our home; and (5) why you should support my desire to buy a speedboat.

A variation of this technique would be to imagine that you are an attorney who has just been hired by your spouse to represent him or her on several areas of conflict between the two of you. Again, no matter how distasteful you find your partner's point of view, take it on like a lawyer would and develop as many arguments as possible in support of your spouse's position, even if it is a defense of obnoxious and/or irresponsible behavior. Remember, the goal here is to develop empathy for your spouse, not to agree with a position you find objectionable. By strengthening your empathy, however, you will be better able to understand where your partner is "coming from." A deeper and more empathic understanding of your spouse's position on points of conflict will either help you change yourself to accommodate to your spouse and give your spouse more of what he or she wants, lead you to consider more compromise solutions, or help you decide to end the relationship without anger and bitterness.

For the sake of review, keep in mind these eight attractive communication behaviors (see Table 3–2, p. 68) each day. If you use all the skills consistently, you will likely see some shift in your partner's interest and availability for problem solving. These attractive communication behaviors will generally lead to more productive meetings with your spouse, reduce defensiveness and arguing, and make it possible to consider problems within a positive, sane atmosphere.

TECHNIQUES TO REDUCE CONFLICT DURING DISCUSSIONS

Despite your best efforts to use attractive communication behaviors and attitudes, discussions with your spouse will sometimes start to flare up into counterproductive arguments. The techniques discussed in this section are designed to stop conflicts from escalating into major "blowouts" between you and your partner.

1. *Admit when you are wrong, have made a mistake or have behaved in an irresponsible/obnoxious manner.* When your spouse levels criticism at you, the first thing to do is ask yourself, "Does my partner have a point? Have I screwed up in some way?" If your answer is yes, then muster the courage to admit it. Nothing diffuses tension better than acknowledging and admitting a mistake, offering an apology, and promising to use your mistake to change future behavior.

You do not need to become defensive when you admit mistakes to yourself and your partner because, as you now know, your worth as a person is not in question—ever! You are a fallible human who does many things well but who also screws up now and then. Admit it! By admitting your mistakes in life without putting yourself down, you learn to rate your behavior as good or bad but not yourself as good or bad. You are always worthwhile, no matter how many mistakes you make.

2. *Talk about the dysfunctional process between you and your spouse.* It sometimes happens that husbands and wives begin

to discuss problems in a calm, sane manner only to find that within minutes tensions are rising, voices are getting louder, and a full-blown argument is brewing. When this happens, try to shift from what you are talking about to *how* you are relating dysfunctionally to each other. The goal of a "content-to-process shift" is to help you and your spouse stand back, see where you're headed, regain control, and then try again to solve the problem without having to go through a major argument. For example, Jack and Lisa found themselves discussing whether Jack should buy a new car, which he very much wanted. Lisa took the position that they could not afford a new car now, and Jack disagreed. Within minutes Jack became red in the face, started to raise his voice, and Lisa began to accuse Jack of having irresponsible spending habits. At this point Jack or Lisa might break their dysfunctional interaction by saying something like, "Look, we're getting very angry at each other and we're not saying helpful things right now. Let's take a break, cool down, and try again to discuss this issue in an hour or so." By making this type of content-to-process shift, you and your spouse can remain vigilant to the signs of emotional disturbance developing and head such disturbance off at the pass. By the way, taking a break to cool down is not the same as changing the subject. After you and your spouse have cooled off, be sure to get back to the specific problem you're trying to solve.

3. *Set limits on your spouse's inappropriate behavior during discussions.* If your husband or wife starts to display verbally abusive or obnoxious behavior during a discussion and won't stop, it is then time for you to set limits and refuse to con-

tinue the discussion until your spouse regains control of his or her emotions and behavior. Set limits in a sincere, kind, and firm manner. You might say something like, "Bob, I really want to solve this problem but I'm not going to talk to you when you're calling me names and yelling at me. Let me know when you're really ready to talk." You then leave the room.

Keep in mind that when you set limits in this way your spouse may try every trick under the sun to get you to join in the fight. Your partner may hurl insults, lay a guilt trip on you, accuse you of being a quitter, and so forth. Resist and ignore all such garbage and manipulative behavior by your spouse. If you do not resist the urge to argue and do allow yourself to be drawn into a loud screaming match, you and your spouse will be acting like 3-year-old children in adult bodies and, like little children, will stand very little chance of solving your problems. The yelling and screaming in your home will also greatly frighten your own children, and you will be acting as poor role models on how to deal with life's problems.

4. Agree to disagree. Sometimes couples reach an impasse on an issue. That is, they find themselves deadlocked with opposing views on how to solve a problem. Both individuals are usually reasonable people with reasonable arguments to support their differing points of view, and neither one wants to give in or compromise. When this situation develops, it is time to agree to disagree for the immediate future. It is rare that couples remain deadlocked on issues forever. As a tactic to buy time to further sort out thoughts, feelings, and possible solutions, the temporary solution of agreeing to disagree often reduces the tensions of the moment and allows each of you the opportunity to peacefully coexist, even if you have different ideas. If you think this is an impossible task, just think about how many Catholics are married to Protestants or Republicans to Democrats. If they can peacefully coexist in the face of fairly large differences, can't you and your spouse agree to disagree over your relatively minor problems?

In this chapter you have learned a number of important ideas about communication as well as eight attractive communication behaviors that you can start using today to improve your marriage. You have also learned four tactics to prevent discussions with your spouse from escalating into major arguments. If you begin using all these methods right away, you will probably see some change in your spouse over the next several weeks. Now that you have worked on these issues, let's move on to the next chapter, developing a repertoire of attractive behavior skills to improve your marriage.

KEY POINTS TO REMEMBER

1. If you really *do not* want to solve your marital problems, keep using the following *unattractive* communication behaviors: threats, ultimatums, dredging up the past, personal attacks, minimizing your partner's point of view, guilt trips, changing the topic, emotional abandonment, and zapping.

2. If you sincerely *want* to solve your marital problems, practice the following *attractive* communication behaviors: show interest in your partner's point of view, actively listen to your partner, use "I" sentences, clarify issues, paraphrase your spouse's ideas, give constructive feedback to your husband or wife, be clear, direct, and to the point, and show empathy for your partner's perspective.

3. To reduce conflict during discussions with your husband or wife, admit when you are wrong, talk about dysfunctional processes that develop during talks, set limits in a kind way on your spouse's inappropriate or abusive behavior, and agree to disagree.

Attractive Behavioral Tactics to Improve Your Marriage

$\mathcal{T}$hink back to the last time you felt a burst of loving feeling toward your husband or wife. Chances are those feelings developed when your partner displayed kind and considerate behavior toward you, helped you solve a problem, or supported one of your goals in life. In other words, your spouse's love behavior probably produced a significant change in your attitude toward him or her and probably also increased your desire to be a cooperative partner. Likewise, your behavior toward your spouse plays a huge role in how he or she feels about you at any given point in time. If you behave in lovable ways toward your partner, he or she will likely experience a burst of good feeling toward you and will want to stay with you. If you act or behave in unlovable ways, your spouse will probably begin to fall out of love with you and may ultimately leave you for someone else. Remember, it is what you *do* for your partner in relation to his or her deepest desires and needs that creates and sustains a deep and lasting emotional bond between the two of you and makes your marriage more secure. The goal of this chapter is to teach you several specific lovable behavioral tactics that you can employ right now to start to improve your marriage and win cooperation from your spouse (Table 4–1). The behaviors described in the following pages represent the behavioral manifestations of human love. Men and women are equally able to use all the following techniques if they *choose* to.

Before you begin to use the attractive behavioral techniques described in the following pages, you first need to decide that you will change your behavior whether or not your spouse changes his or her behavior. If you refuse to change your behavior until your partner changes, you will make very little progress toward your goal of improving your marriage and you will feel like your life is being held hostage by that uncooperative mate of yours. So again, let me state emphatically, work at changing yourself into a saner, calmer person who displays many lovable behaviors toward your spouse. If your spouse is not impressed with the "new you," there are many other people on the planet who will find the "new you"

Table 4–1. Behavioral Tactics to Improve Your Marriage

1. Be a role model
2. Do three pleasurable tasks for your spouse each week
3. Comment on what your husband or wife does well
4. Be kind and nurturing to your spouse's children
5. Playfully offer sexual favors
6. Give your partner space
7. Lovingly touch your partner
8. Stay healthy and physically fit

very attractive. But don't give up on your marriage yet. Do all you can to make it work.

Also, by way of further introduction to the material in this chapter and for the sake of contrast, I want to quickly review the most unlovable, unattractive, self-defeating, marriage-destroying behaviors you could possibly display. In a nutshell they are:

yelling	hitting
moping	breaking property
controlling	pouting
sulking	brooding
guilt-tripping	threatening
name calling	put-downs
manipulating	emotional abandonment
nagging	whining

If you want to make your marriage miserable and thoroughly disgust your mate, keep displaying all these behaviors. If, on the other hand, you want to improve your marriage, give up these infantile behaviors and consider trying some of the following tactics.

1. Be a role model and treat your spouse the way you want to be treated. Being a good role model means practicing what you preach. Thus, if you want more respect, tolerance, co-operation, love, support, and kindness from your spouse, it is critically important for you to display these behaviors and attitudes toward your husband or wife frequently. By doing so you will likely stir or awaken in your partner a burst of good feeling toward you that will help motivate your spouse to give you more of what you want. To better appreciate this key point think back to the last time you encountered an individual who treated you in a friendly, kind, and supportive manner. If you are like most humans you probably reacted with genuinely warm feelings toward that person. By displaying kindness, support, love, and cooperation toward your spouse, you will likely elicit in him or her softer and warmer feelings toward you. A final point about being a good role model and practicing what you preach is that it will also greatly benefit your children.

2. *Do at least three pleasurable tasks for your spouse each week.* Before you start to provide pleasure services to your partner, ask him or her to write down a list of favorite nonsexual pleasures (McKay et al. 1994). You can then use your partner's list of "pleasers" to guide you to provide the specific pleasures your spouse will find meaningful and will likely interpret as your love in action. Again, your spouse loves what you do for him or her more than he or she loves "you" in a general or global sense. Also be sure to keep providing nonsexual pleasure services to your spouse whether or not he or she is able to reciprocate. Do not make your progress contingent upon change in your spouse. By practicing how to provide simple pleasures to your partner, you will definitely make yourself into a more attractive person. In Chapter 6 you will learn what to do if after a reasonable amount of time your partner refuses to cooperate or respond to your pleasure services. For

now just start using this technique and hope for the best. Table 4–2 displays a list of possible nonsexual pleasures that your spouse might enjoy.

3. *Comment on what your spouse does well.* Men and women are equally responsive to positive feedback and praise. By praising your spouse's responsible behaviors frequently, you will probably stir in him or her a heightened desire to give you more of what you want. Throughout each day try to notice and praise your partner for what he or she does well and, as much as possible (not totally), ignore the low-level negative behaviors. Forcefully work with yourself to incorporate words and phrases like "thanks," "good job," "I appreciate your help," and so forth into your daily discussions with your hus-

---

Table 4–2. Ideas to Please Your Spouse

1. Cook a favorite food
2. Give back or foot rub
3. Give hugs and praise
4. Take him or her out to dinner
5. Work out together
6. Let him or her sleep late on weekend
7. Offer to do an errand
8. Play favorite music
9. Go for a walk together
10. Clean the kitchen
11. Pick up around the house
12. Prepare a breakfast in bed
13. Send flowers, for no particular reason
14. Do an extra chore
15. Offer a drink, robe, and slippers
16. Show interest in his or her hobbies

---

band or wife. By doing so you will also be perceived by your partner as a more positive and upbeat person.

4. Be kind and nurturing to your children or your spouse's children. If you have children in your home they will provide you with endless opportunities to improve your relationship with your spouse. Whether they are your biological children or your stepchildren, you will always win points with your spouse by showing love, kindness, and tenderness toward the children. One of the deepest human desires shared by normal men and women is the desire to protect and nurture children. By spending time with your children and caring for them you will very likely elicit in your spouse deep feelings of respect for you and a greater willingness to respond to your desires. And your children will love and respect you as well. There is no down side to becoming deeply involved in the care of the children in your home.

5. Playfully offer sexual favors to your mate. The idea of offering sexual favors to your mate is a delicate issue since there are many factors or variables that affect sexual desire and arousal in humans. Typical variables include mood, stress level, feelings about the body, your inhibitions or lack thereof, feelings about your mate, religious beliefs, what type of early sex education you received, and so forth. The behavioral tactic of making yourself available to sexually pleasure your partner should only be used if you and your spouse are on good enough terms that sexual involvement seems reasonable and desirable. This tactic will likely not be helpful if you and your spouse are at war or in the face of ongoing abusive treatment from each other. Serious situations such as these should be addressed in marital therapy with a qualified mental health professional.

In my view most normal men and women are equally interested in having satisfying love/sex relationships with their partners. It is often the case, however, that couples begin to drift apart sexually, either because of emotional tensions between them or because they simply stop making time for sex when life is busy and hectic. Either way some married people ultimately find themselves in the peculiar position of being married and celibate, which is not exactly what they had in mind when they decided to marry. Unless you and your spouse have agreed to live like roommates, lack of sex in marriage is a risk factor for having your mate lose interest in you. If you are one of those married but nearly celibate individuals, it is within your power to take the initiative to rekindle the bedroom fires with your partner. By doing so you will likely strengthen your mate's interest in and attachment to you, and you might actually begin to have a good sex life again. Love *making* means just that. *You work to make the love and sex you want.*

By now you certainly know what your partner likes to do or not do in the bedroom and what really turns him or her on. Your partner might prefer a nice conversation over dinner and lots of soft, gentle foreplay before intercourse. On the other hand, he or she might like to enact some favorite sexual fantasy or simply have a quick orgasm by any of the standard methods. On a regular basis (you determine the frequency), playfully and lovingly make a sexual offer to your spouse that he or she hopefully will not be able to refuse because it will be an offer to have sex the way your partner likes it. To approach your mate you might say something like, "Honey, would you like to make love tonight? We can do it your way." Most humans enjoy the thought of being sexually pleasured by their partner and find it hard to resist such an offer. If your partner accepts the offer, then deliver the pleasures with love and enthusiasm and with no strings attached, that is, with no expectation of your partner having to do anything for you sexually or otherwise. (Hopefully, your partner will want to return the favors.) If your partner declines your offer, do not upset, anger, or depress yourself about being rejected sexually. Be a good sport about being turned down. Your worth as a person or as a good sexual partner is not on the line. To be a good sport about sexual rejection you might say something like, "You're not in the mood? OK, maybe later in the week we can get together."

Try to offer sexual favors to your mate at times when you are reasonably in the mood for sex and when tensions between you and your spouse have eased a bit. Do not offer sex when you are upset with your spouse or if the thought of sex really turns you off. Also, in trying to meet your partner's sexual desires, offer only those sexual experiences that you can comfortably tolerate or that you might actually enjoy. Do not offer to engage in sexual behaviors that you would experience as humiliating, degrading, disgusting, or that could be harmful to the marital relationship. With these guidelines in mind, look for some regular opportunity to sexually pleasure your partner. The opportunity is there if you take the time and the initiative to make it happen.

To make your sexual pleasure services to your spouse have even greater impact on him or her it is helpful to approach sexual encounters with your mate with playfulness, energy, and enthusiasm. Your strong and enthusiastic desire to make love to your partner is a definite turn-on to him or her. Also, focus on pleasure, not performance. Great sex does not have to be Olympic sex. You do not have to have multiple orgasms, wild gymnastics, or all-nighters for sex to be wonderful. Concentrate on the exquisite sensations that you and your spouse can produce in each other using any combination of body part contacts. Finally, it is also helpful to approach lovemaking with confidence about your worth as a person and your ability to sexually pleasure your mate. Confidence is sexy.

6. *Give your partner space.* Men and women are equally appreciative of having space to think, read, go for a walk, go to bed, or simply decompress. Each day try to gauge whether your partner might prefer some alone time and try to make it possible for him or her to have that time. By actively blocking your urge to talk, problem solve, or interact, you will create space for your partner and by so doing will likely be viewed by him or her as a more supportive mate.

It is not uncommon for wives and husbands to have different levels of interest in sex. In this situation unpleasant tensions sometimes develop when the partner who is less interested in sex feels constantly pressured for sex by the partner with stronger sexual desire. If you generally have more sexual interest than your spouse, try to live with a little less sex and give your mate some space in this area of your relationship. By doing so your husband or wife will likely appreciate your self-restraint and may perhaps even begin to feel that there is now room to initiate sexual contact with you.

7. *Touch your partner in loving ways—often.* Throughout life the gentle caresses of our parents, children, close friends, and lovers reassure, nurture, and soothe us and strengthen our sense of security in love relationships. Each day give your partner hugs, kisses, a pat on the back, or some other form of loving physical contact. Expressing your love in this way will increase your partner's sense of satisfaction about being married to you. A single gentle touch can sometimes say more than any number of words.

8. *Stay healthy and physically fit.* By getting regular exercise and eating a healthy diet you will have more energy and very likely improve your mood as well. Also, the self-love and self-respect reflected through maintenance of your health and fitness will probably be viewed by your spouse as admirable qualities in your personality. Although health, fitness, and physical appearance are not the most important factors in male–female relationships, they do have a role to play in your overall attractiveness to your partner.

KEY POINTS TO REMEMBER

1. If you want to make yourself unattractive to your mate and push him or her away from you, continue to use

the following behaviors: yelling, screaming, whining, pouting, moping, the silent treatment, sulking, threatening, name calling, swearing, emotional abandonment, hitting, and throwing things.

2. If you want to make yourself attractive to your spouse and increase his or her attraction to you, display the following love behaviors frequently: be a role model and treat your partner the way you want to be treated, do three pleasurable tasks for your spouse each week, comment on what your spouse does well, be kind to your partner's children, playfully offer sexual favors to your mate, lovingly touch your partner, and maintain your health and physical fitness.

CHAPTER
5

❧

Attractive Conflict Resolution Skills

Now the stage is set to practice conflict resolution skills. Mastering the art of conflict resolution will increase your attractiveness to your spouse and will likely help you get more of what you want out of your marriage. In this chapter you will learn four ground rules for resolving conflicts with your spouse and a five-step method you can use to negotiate solutions to your marital problems. Now that you have transformed yourself into a thoroughly undisturbable person, you will be able to remain cool, calm, and collected as you and your partner begin to negotiate settlements to your problems.

THE FOUR GROUND RULES
OF CONFLICT RESOLUTION

1. Your partner's point of view is as valid as your point of view. It is imperative that you understand this point. Your spouse feels just as strongly about his or her ideas and feelings as you do about yours. And your partner's point of view is no better or worse than yours. Successful negotiators understand this key point and use this knowledge to approach negotiations with the utmost respect for the other person's point of view. When your spouse realizes that you truly understand and respect that his or her point of view is as valid as yours, you will be more likely to keep your negotiating sessions on the high road of respect, support, and mutual understanding. If you go into a negotiating session holding rigidly to the idea that your partner's point of view is not as valid or as important as yours, you will likely soon end up in a fight with a spouse who is struggling to be taken seriously.

2. *Do not issue threats, personal attacks, or ultimatums when negotiating with your partner.* When trying to solve problems, men and women are equally displeased by cornering tactics, personal attacks, and ultimatums. Strategies such as these will lead your partner to become defensive and to strike back with personal attacks and ultimatums aimed at you. When you feel so frustrated that you are on the brink of "losing it" with your spouse, tell yourself, "I don't like the way this negotiating session is going but I can handle it." "I'm not going to attack or corner my partner. That will only make it less likely that I will be able to get what I want."

3. *Take a break if discussions with your spouse become heated and counterproductive.* Once the volume of your voice has started to go up and the veins in your neck are beginning to

throb it's time to take a short time-out to cool down. When you become this steamed over a conflict with your partner, it means that you are probably thinking in a demanding way and that you are taking the problem, whatever it is, far too seriously. You do not have to become emotionally disturbed over a conflict with your spouse, though it is perfectly normal to feel frustrated, annoyed, and concerned. Use the time-out period to undisturb yourself so that you can resume negotiations with your partner in a more productive and self-helping frame of mind.

4. Be prepared to compromise. It is fine for you to go into negotiating sessions with your spouse hoping (not demanding) to persuade him or her to fully accept your recommended solution to the problem you are trying to solve. If you can get your way, terrific—more power to you. If, however, it looks as though you are not going to exactly get your way, be prepared to compromise. In fact it is generally a good idea to consider ahead of time (that is, before you begin to talk to your partner) what your fallback position might be. In other words, have a Plan A, Plan B, and Plan C in mind. You should even be prepared to let your spouse's point of view carry the day. To be able to think like this and to make negotiations with your partner work, you have to be a flexible thinker. If you remain rigid and unbending in your problem-solving efforts, you will probably experience more unhappiness in your marriage than would be the case if you were a more flexible and tolerant person.

Now that you have these ground rules firmly in mind, let's move on to examine a five-step method of conflict resolution discussed by Bloomquist (1996) for use with children, families, and couples.

THE CONFLICT RESOLUTION PROCEDURE

The following conflict resolution method is straightforward and easy to use. The five steps are:

1. defining the problem
2. proposing possible solutions
3. selecting the most reasonable plan
4. trying the plan
5. evaluating whether the plan worked

Define the Problem Clearly

To start the negotiating session with your partner it is helpful to state clearly the specific problem you are trying to solve. Examples of problems experienced by many couples are such things as how to spend more time together, how to budget or spend money, how to get the house cleaned up, how to manage and raise the children, how to deal with problematic in-laws, and so forth. Whatever the issue, define it clearly and let your partner know in advance of your negotiating session what specific problem you would like to try to solve later when the two of you sit down for the problem-solving discussion. By clearly defining the problem and giving your partner advance notice of the issue, you also give your spouse time to mentally prepare for the meeting and hopefully to develop his or her own Plan A, Plan B, and Plan C.

Propose As Many Solutions As Possible, No Matter How Ridiculous

After you have defined the problem you want to solve, you and your partner should generate a long list of possible solutions. It is absolutely permissible, even desirable, to put a few silly or ridiculous ideas on the solution list. By placing absurd or extreme ideas on the list, it is likely that you and your spouse will quickly be able to experience agreement about ideas you do not want to use. Thus, an atmosphere of collaboration and cooperation is quickly established that hopefully will influence a willingness on both sides to work out a viable compromise solution.

Select a Plan

The next step in problem solving is to select the solution or plan that is most agreeable to you and your partner. Whatever plan you agree to (whether you won, lost, or compromised), it is important that you support the plan consistently and enthusiastically. Tell yourself, "I will do my best to make this plan work. It is important that my spouse and I learn to work together to make our solutions work."

Implement the Plan

The implementation phase involves some discussion of who will do what and when. It might be helpful to write down the specific details of the plan so that you and your partner will be more likely to remember what you have each agreed to do to make the plan work. This is the stage of problem solving that involves hard work, persistence of effort, and sweat to transform the idea of a solution into reality.

Evaluate the Effectiveness of the Plan

After you have selected a plan and agreed to the details of implementation, it is important to set aside a time two to four weeks later to review how satisfied you and your spouse are with the results of the plan. By setting up a future review meeting, you and your spouse create a forum to assess the effectiveness of the plan, make minor adjustments to the plan if necessary, or scrap the plan altogether and create new ideas to solve the problem.

EXAMPLE OF CONFLICT RESOLUTION

For months Kathy and Vincent have been arguing about house cleaning. Kathy thinks that she does too much picking up around the house and that Vincent does not do his fair share. Vincent is working long hours at his job and wants to be able to relax when he comes home and to play golf on the weekends. Vincent thinks Kathy is not being sympathetic to his desire for relaxation. The intensity of the screaming matches over house cleaning indicate that Kathy and Vincent have become emotionally disturbed about this area of dissatisfaction in their relationship. To solve this problem, Kathy and

Vincent first take personal responsibility for their respective self-defeating emotional reactions and work vigorously to become undisturbed about the house cleaning problem. Once they calm themselves down to a level of appropriate self-helping annoyance and frustration, they agree to sit down and try a new problem-solving method.

1. Defining the problem. Kathy says, "Vincent, I'm frustrated by having to do all the housework. I'd like to sit down this evening to see if we can come up with a plan to share the work." Vincent agrees to talk later, and he begins to think about how he might be able to help his wife with this problem.

2. Creating a list of possible solutions. At the start of the meeting the specific problem to be solved is restated, and a list of possible solutions is developed. After about ten minutes Kathy and Vincent have created the following list of possible solutions:

1. Hire a maid to do all the house work.
2. Throw most of the contents of the house out so that cleaning and picking up won't be necessary.
3. Let the house become messy and ignore it.
4. Move to an efficiency apartment where cleaning will be easier.
5. Kathy will do laundry and dishes and keep the bathroom clean. Vincent will do vacuuming and dusting and will put the trash out.
6. Vincent will do all the cleaning for one month, then Kathy will do all the cleaning for one month.

7. Kathy will do all the cleaning on Mondays, Tuesdays, Wednesdays, and Thursdays. Vincent will do all the cleaning on Fridays, Saturdays, and Sundays.

3. *Selecting the most reasonable plan.* At this stage Kathy and Vincent go through the list and weigh the pros and cons of each option. Very quickly they agree that options 1, 2, 3, 4, and 6 are out. They now weigh the advantages and disadvantages of options 5 and 7. After some additional discussion, Vincent and Kathy agree on option 5. Kathy will be responsible for laundry, dishes, and keeping the bathroom clean. Vincent will take care of vacuuming, dusting, and taking the trash out.

4. *Implementing the plan.* Next Kathy and Vincent work out the details of the plan. Kathy agrees to do the dishes every day, do the laundry two times per week, and clean the bathroom one time per week. Vincent agrees to take the trash out on Saturday and Thursday evenings and vacuum and dust the house one time per week. Vincent also agrees to put his dirty clothes in the hamper every day. Both agree to work hard to make the plan succeed. After arranging these details, Vincent and Kathy agree to meet again in three weeks to talk about how the plan is working.

5. *Evaluating the effectiveness of the plan.* Three weeks later Vincent and Kathy meet as agreed. During the discussion they realize that the house work has been getting done as planned and that they have rarely been arguing. Kathy says that the distribution of work seems fair to her. Vincent says that he

has actually been enjoying his golf game more since he no longer feels guilty about avoiding his fair share of house work. They agree that the plan is working and decide to keep it going.

KEY POINTS TO REMEMBER

1. To negotiate effectively, remember that your spouse's point of view is as valid as your point of view.

2. Do not issue threats, personal attacks, or ultimatums during problem-solving discussions.

3. Take breaks when problem-solving talks become heated.

4. Be prepared to compromise.

5. To resolve a conflict with your husband or wife, define the problem clearly, propose many possible solutions, select a solution, implement the solution, and after two or three weeks evaluate whether the solution worked.

6. If your solution did not work, start over again using the same conflict resolution method to develop a new plan to solve your problem.

7. If your solution did work, reward yourself and your spouse. Go out to dinner and a movie.

What To Do If Your Spouse Just Won't Cooperate

$\mathcal{A}$t the beginning of this book I stated that real love delivers attitudes of kindness, cooperation, and understanding. You did not get married to live a life of frustration, upset, loneliness, or embarrassment over your spouse's inconsiderate, self-centered, abusive, or otherwise obnoxious behaviors. You married for companionship, love, mutual support, and kindness. In short, you married to have a "soul mate" with whom you would share life's joys and frustrations. If you have worked hard to use what you have learned in this book and have not seen improvement in your marriage, it is time to get tough with your partner in ways that will let him or her know you are dead serious about wanting change in your marriage. In this chapter you will learn several get-tough strategies that will hopefully serve as wake-up calls to your husband or wife.

GETTING TOUGH WITH KINDNESS

If at this point you remain frustrated in your efforts to win cooperation from your spouse, it might be time to develop a more intense action plan to capture your spouse's attention and hopefully motivate him or her to change. Although you may have started to feel helpless and hopeless in regard to your marital problems, you do in fact have power and control over many things that will affect your partner. For example, you control many valued services in your home such as running errands, paying bills, doing laundry, shopping for food, cooking, doing lawn work, cleaning, and doing house maintenance and repairs. The way to get tough with your partner is to stop providing the services you typically provide, but always with an attitude of kindness, never out of hatred, anger, bitterness, or resentment.

Before you implement your action plan there are a few ground rules to consider. First, it is important to give your spouse fair warning about your get-tough action plan. Let your partner know that you are still very concerned about the lack of cooperation and that if there is no change in behavior and attitude within one week you will no longer cook, clean, pay bills, shop, do laundry, or whatever for him or her. By announcing your plan to stop services ahead of time, you will appear rational and in control of your emotions. If you were to suddenly and emotionally spring your action plan on your spouse, he or she might not take you seriously and instead might think of you as an impulsive, irrational person. If after you have announced your plan to stop services your spouse still chooses not to cooperate, it is imperative that you follow through and do what you said you would do. If you do not follow through with your plan to stop services, you will lose all credibility with your partner and he or she will be even less likely to change. A second key point is that you strive to maintain an attitude of friendliness, kindness, and sincerity when you announce your action plan and when you actually implement the plan. Remember, the goal of this technique is to save your marriage, not destroy it with hate, bitterness, revenge, and anger. Third, it is important to consider whether you are in any danger of physical abuse by your partner. If you think that getting tough with your spouse could actually put you at risk for abusive treatment, you should seek professional help right away. If this is what you are living with, your marriage is much too troubled for this technique to be helpful, and it might actually make your situation worse, which is something I do not want to have happen. Finally, whatever action steps you take vis-à-vis your spouse, be sure they do not adversely affect your children.

Examples of the Warning of the Action Plan

Karina says to Miguel, "I continue to be unhappy about how much time you are out with your friends. I really want us to have more time together. If by next Monday you are unable to respond to what I want, I will start to make my life a little easier by no longer cooking or cleaning for you or doing your laundry. I genuinely hope we can resolve this problem before next week, but if not I will absolutely stop performing these services for you."

Robert says to Laura, "I'm very concerned about how much money you have been spending and your unwillingness to stick to our budget. If you choose not to work with me on this issue, starting on Friday I will no longer take out the

*trash, mow the lawn, or do the weekly shopping. I will also
no longer pay the bills that come in your name."*

Robert and Karina had better be prepared to follow through
on these action plans even though it may be emotionally difficult to do so. Sometimes getting tough (with kindness) and
setting limits are the only ways to get through to a difficult
partner.

WHAT TO DO IF YOUR SPOUSE
STILL WON'T COOPERATE

If your spouse still does not respond to your concerns and
your action plan, you should make an appointment with a
licensed mental health professional for additional help on
your marital problems. Perhaps in the context of individual
therapy for yourself you will be able to develop additional
strategies to win cooperation from your spouse, or possibly
persuade him or her to attend marital counseling sessions
with you.

If psychotherapy for you alone or you and your partner
together produces no results and you are still unhappy in your
marriage, it might be time to concede that you and your husband or wife simply were not meant to be together. In other
words, the two of you are so mismatched it is unlikely that any
amount of work will get your marriage back on track. The two
of you are like oil and water. You just don't mix. If you have
come to the conclusion that you and your partner were not
meant to be together, it does not mean that men and women

are from different planets. It simply means that you and your spouse are two Earthlings who are incompatible. That is, one or both of you continuously *chooses* not to do what it takes to make your marriage work. Too bad, that's the way it is.

It is not for me to tell you how to live your life or what you should do about an unhappy marriage. Some individuals actually choose to stay in miserable marriages for economic reasons or allegedly for the sake of the children, although children suffer enormously by living with two unhappy or angry parents. I will, however, share with you what I would do if I were in a miserable relationship with my spouse.

If I were chronically unhappy and frustrated with my spouse and had made repeated good-faith efforts to improve the marriage with no success, I would with genuine sorrow and regret (not horror, rage, or despair) initiate divorce proceedings. I would do so with kindness and respect toward my spouse. I would work with myself to remember that my spouse is a fallible human being who simply was not interested in the same things that interested me. I would forgive my partner for past bad or obnoxious behavior but would remind myself that my soon-to-be ex-spouse is always a worthwhile human being. For the sake of the children, I would strive to remain an effective parent and would make a solemn commitment to work cooperatively with my ex-spouse on any issues concerning the care of the children. And I would never "bad mouth" my child's other parent. This, in a nutshell, is what I would do if I were in a miserable marriage. Once I had grieved the loss of this important relationship, I would then optimistically look to the future and set out to find another mate with whom I could share my life.

It is my sincere hope that the problem-solving methods you have learned in this book have by now produced positive changes in your relationship with your spouse. If not, and you have decided to end your marriage, keep in mind that someone out there is very likely to be turned on by the attractive new you. Billions of male and female humans inhabit our planet. If the male or female you picked this time is not right for you, don't despair. It is very likely you will meet a new love partner at some point. But even if you don't meet someone else you can still enjoy many other pleasures in life, such as friends, good books, travel, music, movies, work, and so forth, and not be preoccupied with problems stemming from a bad marriage.

In any event, I want to congratulate you on your efforts to improve yourself and your marriage. Developing new habits, behaviors, attitudes, and problem-solving methods is not an easy task. But if you keep at it and continue to use all the relationship-enhancing techniques I have discussed, you and your spouse are likely to develop an increasingly loving relationship. It really is possible for women and men to enjoy life together. I hope all goes well for you and your partner in life.

KEY POINTS TO REMEMBER

1. Announce your get-tough action plan one week ahead of time and then follow through on the plan if you do not see change in your partner.

2. When you implement your action plan, do so with kindness and respect for your partner.

3. Your action plan preferably should involve a withholding of the regular services you provide for your husband or wife, such as cooking, cleaning, house repairs, yard work, laundry, errands, and so forth.

4. If you decide to end your marriage, it is unlikely that you will be alone for the rest of your life.

5. If the methods in this book have helped you win cooperation from your spouse, keep using them far into the future.

ᗷ Appendix ᗷ
Guidelines for Clinicians

Though primarily a self-help book for married individuals, this book is also designed to support any marital therapy effort or any type of individual therapy for a married person who is seeking to improve his or her marriage. It can be used simply as recommended reading for clients who wish to facilitate self-improvement in marriage as well as relational improvement with the spouse, or it can be used as a structured, step-by-step intervention for distressed couples. Either way, both the psychoeducational content of this book and the emotional and interpersonal problem-solving methods it prescribes are likely to help many unhappily married individuals decisively end the marital "madness" and create more satisfying relationships with their partners.

My view of relational disorders is greatly influenced by the work of Dr. Albert Ellis and his colleagues at the Albert Ellis Institute for Rational Emotive Behavior Therapy in New York City. The Rational Emotive Behavior Therapy (REBT) theory

of relationship disturbance focuses mainly on the two individuals in the marital dyad and their respective irrational
beliefs toward each other as opposed to only family of origin
issues or only current family dynamics and structure. Although I occasionally weave psychodynamic, family systems,
or psychoanalytic interventions into my work with couples, I
largely rely on REBT methods and generally find them to be
efficient and effective. To learn more about the REBT approach to marital therapy, I recommend a book by Ellis and
co-authors (1989) called *Rational-Emotive Couples Therapy*.

GENERAL CONSIDERATIONS IN CLINICAL WORK WITH COUPLES

In this section I offer a few ideas that I have found to be
particularly helpful in my work with troubled couples or with
unhappily married individuals.

1. In cases where one or both spouses have substance
   abuse and/or psychiatric problems, it is imperative that
   such disorders be treated first. Once problems such as
   these have been successfully addressed, a fresh evaluation of the couple's readiness for marital treatment can
   be conducted.

2. To facilitate a therapeutic alliance with couples, it is
   critical that the therapist remain objective and gender-
   neutral. A clinician who gives in to the natural human
   tendency to identify with or be loyal to persons of the

same gender runs the risk of sabotaging marital therapy. To keep myself gender-neutral, I constantly strive to view my marital therapy clients as two human beings in distress.

3. Be careful *not* to agree with either partner's view that "the problem," whatever it may be, is horrible, terrible, or awful. Remember, the words *horrible, terrible,* and *awful* mean worse than the worst thing that could ever happen to a person. Clinicians who support such distorted evaluations of marital problems actually strengthen irrational thinking in their clients and, by doing so, likely make their clients more disturbed.

4. Many couples can be successfully treated by focusing mainly on the present and the future. I generally spend very little time on past problems or issues. In fact, in many of my marital cases, I do not even gather much historical or family of origin material other than the required basics covered during the evaluation session. Once in a while, a brief detour into the past is helpful, but I do not dwell on the past or allow my clients to dwell on past problems. Instead, I focus on helping couples create a better present for themselves and, hopefully, a brighter marital future.

5. I conceptualize initial sessions with troubled couples as meetings where I conduct individual psychotherapy simultaneously on husband and wife. At this stage, the goal is to help husband and wife surrender their disturbance-

creating, irrational beliefs toward each other and take personal responsibility for their dysfunctional emotions and behaviors. As soon as the individuals in the marital dyad have become less reactive and less emotionally disturbed, I move on to teach them the communication and problem-solving skills they need to sanely address legitimate areas of marital dissatisfaction.

6. In my work with couples and individual clients I do not demand good treatment outcome or compliance with my treatment plan. Instead, I strive to remain preferential regarding the outcome of therapy and client compliance with my recommendations. In other words, I strongly prefer and hope that my clients will apply what I teach them, but they never have to. There is no law of the universe that says I must get the good treatment outcomes or client compliance I want. By thinking this way, I find that I am more relaxed and playful with my clients.

7. It is important to remember that our clients, even our most difficult and troubled ones, are always and unconditionally worthwhile human beings, even when they continue to act in self- or therapy-defeating ways.

A FEW SPECIFIC CONSIDERATIONS

Men Are from Earth, Women Are from Earth can be used as a six-step intervention to promote better and more fulfilling relationships between men and women. Each chapter is designed as a separate relationship-enhancing "module" that provides a focus for discussions in group or individual sessions with couples. This intervention is logically sequenced and easy to follow by client and clinician alike. In the following paragraphs I offer a few clinical tips pertaining to each of the six modules in this book. Keep in mind, however, that there is nothing absolute or dogmatic in the following material. Clinicians should feel free to adapt or modify any aspect of my approach based upon their clinical judgment, creativity, and the individual treatment needs of clients.

Chapter 1—Getting Ready for Change

The main clinical task associated with this chapter is to set the stage for positive change between husband and wife. Though there is much to be discussed in this chapter, it is important to:

1. emphasize that any marriage can work if both individuals are willing to do what it takes to make it work
2. teach couples the difference between marital disturbance and marital dissatisfaction, stressing simultaneously the self-defeating nature of marital disturbance and the legitimacy of each individual's marital dissatisfactions
3. help husband and wife take personal responsibility for their respective relationship-damaging, self-sabotaging emotional and behavioral actions and reactions and

see that their current problem-solving efforts are dysfunctional
4. introduce the idea that forced behavioral change can lead to changes in thinking and feeling
5. help each spouse commit to change whether or not the partner changes.

Chapter 2—How Disturbable Are You?

The central clinical task associated with this chapter is to help husband and wife or the unhappily married individual become strongly feeling yet thoroughly undisturbable persons. To achieve this goal it is necessary to:

1. help clients accept the cornerstone REBT principle that events in the world do not disturb us as much as the way we view or evaluate bad events or difficult situations
2. teach clients Ellis's ABC model of emotional disturbance and emotional problem solving
3. teach clients the difference between healthy and unhealthy negative emotions
4. show clients how to become their own therapists by identifying, disputing, and discarding their irrational beliefs and other forms of problematic thinking
5. recommend that husband and wife commit to a daily review of the rational coping statements listed at the end of this chapter
6. reinforce the idea that changes in thinking can lead to changes in feeling and behavior.

Chapter 3—Attractive Communication Skills

The goal of this module is to teach husband and wife effective self- and relationship-enhancing communication skills. To help a couple develop communication skills, it is important to:

1. remind the couple that words and ideas, no matter how offensive or hard to hear, cannot harm or diminish a person's value one bit
2. review the eight most common dysfunctional forms of communication
3. provide in-session training in clean, attractive communication skills
4. help husband and wife agree to use the four conflict reduction techniques discussed at the end of this chapter.

Chapter 4—Attractive Behavioral Tactics to Improve Your Marriage

The main goal of this stage is to encourage the emergence of love behaviors between husband and wife and to reinforce the idea that men and women tend to love what their spouses *do* for them in relation to their most deeply felt desires. To promote the development of love behavior in marriage, it is advisable to:

1. review the unattractive, marriage-destroying behaviors that men and women commonly display toward one another
2. help each individual commit to behavioral change whether or not the spouse changes

3. encourage the partners to start using a few or all of the love behaviors discussed in this chapter
4. again reinforce the idea that forced behavioral change can lead to significant changes in thought and feeling.

Chapter 5—Attractive Conflict Resolution Skills

This module is designed to give husband and wife the problem-solving tools necessary to resolve or settle many day-to-day problems of living as well as larger issues and conflicts. Though the problem-solving method discussed in this chapter may appear simple, each individual will have to utilize simultaneously the cognitive skills to reduce emotional disturbance learned in Chapter 2 *and* the attractive communication skills discussed in Chapter 3. To promote effective problem solving, it is helpful to:

1. review the four ground rules of conflict resolution between mates
2. teach the couple the five-step problem-solving method described in this chapter
3. encourage in-session practice on minor marital problems or dissatisfactions before allowing its use on larger problems.

Chapter 6—What To Do If Your Spouse Just Won't Cooperate

This chapter shows an unhappily married individual how to get tough with a spouse who just won't cooperate or respond.

To teach the get-tough-with-kindness technique, it is important to:

1. stress that the goal of this tactic is to save, not destroy, the marriage
2. review the ground rules for a get-tough action plan
3. help the individual who is contemplating the use of this technique to identify the specific services he or she will cut off as a wake-up call to the uncooperative spouse. If, at that point, the uncooperative partner is still attending sessions, it is very important that he or she continue to receive equal amounts of support and acceptance from the therapist as well as acknowledgment of his or her frustrations in the marriage.

✄ References ✄

Bloomquist, M. (1996). *Skills Training for Children with Behavior Disorders.* New York: Guilford.

Dryden, W., and DiGiuseppe, R. (1990). *A Primer on Rational-Emotive Therapy.* Champaign, IL: Research Press.

Ellis, A. (1994). *Reason and Emotion in Psychotherapy,* 2nd ed. New York: Carol/Birch Lane.

———— (1996). *Better, Deeper and More Enduring Brief Therapy: The Rational-Emotive Behavior Therapy Approach.* New York: Brunner/Mazel.

Ellis, A., and Dryden, W. (1997). *The Practice of Rational-Emotive Behavior Therapy,* rev. ed. New York: Springer.

Ellis, A., Sichel, J., Yeager, R., et al. (1989). *Rational-Emotive Couples Therapy.* New York: Pergamon.

Hauck, P. (1984). *The Three Faces of Love.* Louisville, KY: Westminster/John Knox.

McKay, M., Fanning, P., and Paleg, K. (1994). *Couple Skills: Making Your Relationship Work*. Oakland, CA: New Harbinger.

Wenning, K. (1996). *Winning Cooperation from Your Child!: A Comprehensive Method to Stop Defiant and Aggressive Behavior in Children*. Northvale, NJ: Jason Aronson.

๛ Suggested Reading ๛

Ellis, A. (1988). *How to Stubbornly Refuse to Make Yourself Miserable About Anything—Yes, Anything!* Secaucus, NJ: Lyle Stuart.

This is a book you should stubbornly refuse to put down until you have finished it. It will give you many insights into the ways in which you needlessly disturb yourself over a variety of life problems. The self-help techniques it contains will also help you gain control of your emotional destiny so that you can maximally enjoy life and have as little emotional pain as possible.

Ellis, A., and Harper, R. A. (1997). *A Guide to Rational Living*, 3rd rev. ed. North Hollywood, CA: Wilshire.

This guide to rational living is one of the most widely read self-help books in the world. In it Drs. Ellis and Harper discuss in detail ten irrational beliefs that cause human psychological disturbance. If you study this book carefully and actively model its self-helping philosophies around your spouse, you will be showing him or her how not to become an emotionally disturbed individual.

Ellis, A., and Tafrate, R. C. (1997). *How to Control Your Anger before It Controls You.* Secaucus, NJ: Carol/Birch Lane. When it comes to a discussion of anger, this book leaves no stone unturned. Throughout the discussion, Drs. Ellis and Tafrate systematically show how you create and maintain your anger by holding rigidly to self-angering philosophies about other people and the world. This book will help you detect and dispute your self-angering philosophies and beliefs, and it will teach you numerous ways to think, feel, and act your way out of an overly angry outlook on life.

Hauck, P. A. (1974). *Overcoming Frustration and Anger.* Philadelphia: Westminster. (Now available through Westminster/John Knox in Louisville, KY.) This is another good book to help you learn about the sources of your anger and to change yourself into a less angry person. In the discussion, Dr. Hauck shows you the complete psychological sequence of getting angry. He also shows how to deal with self-righteous anger and how to stop being so blaming of others. The book concludes with nine specific guidelines for overcoming frustration and anger.

✍ Index ✍

ABOUT THE AUTHOR

Kenneth Wenning received his MSW (1980) and Ph.D. (1988) from the Smith College School for Social Work in Northampton, Massachusetts. For the past sixteen years, he has specialized in the treatment of couples and in the evaluation and treatment of children who are oppositional, defiant, and aggressive. Dr. Wenning maintains a private practice of child, family, and couple treatment in Hamden, Connecticut. He is the author of *Winning Cooperation from Your Child!: A Comprehensive Method to Stop Defiant and Aggressive Behavior in Children.*